DATE DUE

JAMES'S LATER NOVELS

AN INTERPRETATION

What matters, for one's appreciation of a work of art, however modest, is that the prime intention shall have been justified—for any judgment of which we must be clear as to what it was.

—HENRY JAMES

JAMES'S
LATER NOVELS

AN INTERPRETATION

by ROBERT MARKS

THE WILLIAM-FREDERICK PRESS

NEW YORK   1960

MANUFACTURED IN THE UNITED STATES OF AMERICA

COPYRIGHT © 1 9 6 0 BY ROBERT MARKS

Library of Congress Catalog Card Number : 59-6416

THE WILLIAM-FREDERICK PRESS

391 EAST 149TH STREET   NEW YORK 55, N. Y.

CONTENTS

A NOTE

READERS who are familiar with Henry James will observe that many phrases and even longer passages from his writings have been incorporated into the text of this work without any indication of their source. I have fallen back on this expedient because I do not know how else . . .

R.M.

A VISION OF HENRY JAMES

EVERY READER brings to an author's work, as his prime contribution, an individual vision, the special quality of his understanding, a quality which until he speaks remains necessarily vague. If one didn't lend an author something of one's own where would he be? The quantity *read into* a work that makes it give out an interest is to be reckoned with, and for it we have to thank the justifying commentator who spends on it boldly, ingeniously, like a fond investor, to make it pay. And to follow from beginning to end—or as far as either our intelligence or our simplemindedness permits—any claim to interest or convince us by "radical reinterpretation," any discharge upon those wondrous creations of James's thoroughly mature and highly developed period of some brisk shower of general ideas, is to be reminded afresh that we are in presence of work that has a remarkable capacity for absorbing or accommodating ideas; and if the supreme sign of the critics who have hitherto undertaken to expose their inferential meaning is just that they have been mostly romantic, the supreme sign of the elucidated pages is just that they are hospitable to those ideas that these critics have liked.

What most previous explainers have shown to be in these late novels has required for its discovery a certain way of looking, a mode of seeing that which is otherwise invisible. Collectively they have held up a torch revealing, with a luridness, in what romantic darkness regarding Henry James oneself has for the most part walked, and in the flare of which familiar characters and incidents from the copious artistry of his later years, so lighted, take on a newness of aspect, of interest and importance. One had seen these matters primarily as so other. And the object of this batch of résumés or abstracts or whatever is to present an attitude or aspect

9

that is curiously different and the force of which has not yet been generally felt; to put forth complementary to the vision that has been so widely accepted one that has hardly, in the age of criticism and of revived interest in James, got into print at all on a scale to speak of.

There is that which this author gives to his reader and that which he leaves to the reader to bring. The substance finally projected and most desirable is a matter of appreciation, judgment, interpretation in the sense of being a feature of vision as well as of the object. In venturing a single exposition, then, one has the sense of lowering the whole pitch, that of expression, that of interpretation above all: there is the mystification and the amusement of the work being somehow such different things at the same time. But the particular "figure in the carpet" that has most solicited one's own attention has been in contradiction so complete to the one that has vigorously weathered so many seasons making up the history of James criticism, or what passes for such, that there is the ambiguity and the wonder of scarce knowing if these writings most carry their author's vision out or most open themselves to one's own vision; whether meanings read into or meanings read out of predominate. And that is his secret and his joke; with the attitude of irony, so constant in him, that is the pass to which he brought the novel.

One of the theories current to account for his ambiguity is that as he went in life this novelist, who of all novelists was most of one, got more and more lost in the ingenious labyrinth of his own technical constructions and sank progressively deeper into a bewilderment caused by the very multiplicity of his own perceptions, so much so that he presented us at the latter end of his career with pale pages into which we are at liberty to read pretty well whatever sense we can, or whatever meanings we prefer. James was indeed "doubled" if ever a writer was, but that he was so confused isn't, of course, a belief of one's own, nor is it possible that his particular marvelous effects could have been arrived at unconsciously. The ambition of this book is the imputation to him, with an equanimity of confidence, of some ideas—both of life and form—cherished as convictions, those of which his novels and stories are dramatizations and embodiments, supreme ideas and recurrent techniques of his thought that constitute an underlying point of view sharp and bright by which his work all hangs together, which impart to it a unity, a character, a tone, and from which it derives its final value. Philosophically, if you please, they are what the novels ultimately mean: the sense that we shall find in him in the last analysis. Though we don't arrive at the best residuum of his truth by any easy first process, it is the sense within the sense for us to look for.

And once light dawns in this direction, numerous omens and portents can be made out which fit together and harmonize as a coherent pattern, albeit in the indirect and muffled fashion of dramatic essences. Everything depends on the reader's own general vision of things and his sense of what constitutes significations of a determinant character. What is required for these interpretations to respectably involve and accredit and present themselves as such is an imagination open to such advances and satisfied by such a sense. Given the favoring turn of mind, these ideas applied to the novels unlock in them a certain door of importances, a door to their higher truth, if you will, or to the remoter real, the real other than "immediate" and "guaranteed."

To a critic skeptically minded, with a weaker sense for meanings in this sort, it may seem that ideas so communicated become such on rather "easy" terms, unambiguous evidence for them being so little directly producible, though the assurance with which they are presented being on that account not less. To the skeptical vision, doubtless, what is happening all the while is that one is imagining things, quite on system, wholly other than as they are. The implication is that if all this is not quite as one makes it out and represents it one has then succeeded in inventing it as such, and it is oneself who is the artist here! The truth, of course, is much less flattering. There is the sense of the romantic and there is the sense of the real, and to impose upon a mere expositor's too foolishly babbled secrets any such magic of creation is merely to underestimate the quantity of one or the other of these atmospheres that this genius of the first order in the novel had to give out.

With age his talent grew finer and more deeply penetrating both of life and his craft, but so far as these novels of fullest power have penetrated the imagination of the public they have penetrated mostly their romantic part. What one has perhaps succeeded in doing for some then is to spoil and blight the romantic thrill of many of his choicest pages! But to note a series of sketches pretending to do this in a rudimentary way as a thing unprecedented up to this latest season is a sufficient implication that the criticism of our novelist is rather closer to its beginning than its end, that the critical intelligence has not yet really started to render him its finer tribute, and one has had to classify him, for convenience, among the most fortunate: the writers for whom there is still more to come; those for whom their future in the popular affection will be still more beautiful than their past, that happy time when everything they have done will be recognized for what it is.

Over a period of years A. R. Orage, Harold C. Goddard, Edna Kenton, Edmund Wilson, Marius Bewley, and others have pointed out that in *The Turn of the Screw* everything is regulated and exhibited in double and that we so get the rich real and the rich romantic at a stroke, and its appeal to the imagination is thereby doubled. But the popular critical response to this disclosure (insofar as its genuineness has not been questioned, or at least the fact that this effect was planned by its author questioned) has been that *The Turn of the Screw* is an experiment out of the ordinary for James, the only thing of its kind, an anomaly unique in literature and unparalleled in his other work. The fact of course is that *The Turn of the Screw* (of 1898) is just one expressive sample of the technique employed by James generally and methodically in the last phase of his mental progress, a technique that started and developed in the short stories—*The Path of Duty,* of 1884 is an early instance; *Louisa Pallant,* of 1888, is another—and grew there in subtlety until it reached the short novel length with *The Spoils of Poynton,* in 1896, and was a feature of *all* the abundant literary progeny of his mind thereafter. One has failed to note any general awareness of this: the indications have been rather of the failure to see, to comprehend.

No sketch of *The Sacred Fount,* a short novel written in the later technique, has been included, and none of the unfinished novel *The Sense of the Past.* Briefly, the narrator of *The Sacred Fount* is a case of incipient lunacy and the 300-page work is his first-hand report of a weekend spent at an English country house. The thing is a sort of satire on the extra-marital flirtations and combinations that occur at such gatherings and on the accompanying gossip and theorizing about people that takes places. The narrator is affected by a widow there; but she is in covert pursuit of a young married man; he in turn is interested in a young married woman —and so on. The narrator's ideas about these people show a deteriorated sense of reality: they are fantasies in which his wishes attain imaginary fulfillment. But he regards them to be prodigies of perspicacity, and he does have some art of putting things. At the end, one of the women tells him the true facts of the situation and he produces secondary delusions about her to serve for "rationalization." The novel is not as popular as *The Turn of the Screw,* and also probably not as fine. James excluded it from the New York edition. *The Sacred Fount's* narrator suffers in comparison with the governess of the more famous tale in having no recourse to the "supernatural," and also in being cast in a comedy requiring his bafflement for a conclusion—whereas there is no muddlement of this sort at the end of *The Turn of the Screw* to confuse or discomfit the reader.

The expositor's office is to point out, by more or less rude simplifications and cheapenings and explicitnesses, his subject's personal and special message to the world, or at least what he imputes to him to be such. There of course is one, a perfect place for the real planting of the standard and the giving of its folds to the air, the standard that this novelist appears to have so little publicly brandished. And to readers beyond the need or help of such expositions, whatever their numbers, one can only apologize for so much lucidity that is not in their interest. The attempt has been simply to be as plain as possible about James's own supreme clarity, both perceptional and expressional, the eminent clearness of a great and special man of letters, a man who found the philosophy of fiction a chaos and left it a science, a dealer in illusion and delusion as parts of life who was nothing if not articulate and who never failed of either clearness or fullness of sense.

The truth is that James can afford to let his work eloquently plead for itself—it is the nature of artistic intentions to be supremely capable of giving account of themselves—but one has *had* necessarily, in order to retain the pleasure of making "reckless revelations," to stifle whatever qualms come up about expatiating grossly and copiously upon the possibly obvious. One has *had* with more or less grimness to cling to the tradition that the James of the final period is delightfully "difficult" and that one is breaking ground where it had not hitherto, among us, strangely enough, been much broken. There does exist—we see it about us—the Question of Henry James, and it is not every day we meet a novelist about whom there is a question. So one has had fairly to pounce upon this hint to approach the work of his maturer years on paper, for popular explanation and comprehension, as some tract of more or less virgin snow with only here and there the stray footprint of a critic, as a preserve not yet known in all its extent to the investigators, as some aggregation of unprofaned mysteries that even the adventures of the new criticism of our author, so far as there is any, have not yet got round to clearing up. And in James's highly explorable garden one has the sense of pulling at roots intrinsically worth it—strong enough, and fine enough, and entire enough.

THE AWKWARD AGE

JAMES HAS been much abused as a playwright. *The Awkward Age,* which runs to 548 pages in the New York edition, is his longest work in this kind, and also probably his best, but there are others that are also good. Its general subject is female adolescence: the time after a girl finishes with the schoolroom and starts to "come out" in her mother's parlor until the day she is marriageably disposed of. Nanda is our young lady and the interval of tension and apprehension in this case extends from about March of one year to June of the next. There is no concentration of interest in one person, however. In James's famous *nouvelle The Beast in the Jungle,* for instance, the figure of May Bartram is subsidiary to Marcher and drawn flat deliberately; but the characters in *The Awkward Age* are presented in the round. It is a drama of the interactions of a group of people upon each other; it is a picture of relations, among which and on the first line of interest is the relation of Nanda Brookenham to her mother, and also the relation of Mrs. Brookenham to Nanda. And the whole thing is reflected in the talk; no one's mind is gone into for the subjective picturing of emotional states.

THE ROMANCE

The persons portrayed are all English and the setting is England in the 1890s. There are Mrs. Bookenham and her husband. He is in some ways excellent, but he is not particularly imaginative nor energetic, and the couple have too small of an income to keep afloat socially without prodigious labors of contrivance on the part of the wife, who is a marvelously clever woman. The daughter Nanda, upon whom Mrs. Brook (to shorten the name, as the characters themselves do) counts to make an advantageous marriage, is too sentimental to cooperate. The girl is foolish enough, from her mother's point of view, to be in love with Vanderbank, who is handsome, rather than with Mitchy, who is superlatively hideous but rich and who loves her. There is also old Mr. Longdon from Beccles in the country who is visiting London after many years of absence. He was in his youth a great admirer of Mrs. Brook's mother but he does not fancy Mrs. Brook, who strikes him as being too concerned with advancing herself through her daughter. He does, however, like Nanda. So much indeed does he like her that he discreetly informs Vanderbank that he will, in the event of the fellow's marrying her, provide a substantial dowry for her himself.

Van is undecided. He asks Mr. Longdon for time. He talks over the possibility with the girl's mother—with whom he has been having something of an affair. Mrs. Brook's ideals, (a) to marry the young lady to Mitchy's millions, and (b) to reserve Van for herself, remain unshaken by Mr. Longdon's bribe. But a cousin of Mr. Brook has adopted a niece and raised her as a *jeune fille*. "Nanda perceives," one commentator explained, "that the Duchess, her stepmother, is too crude a woman, even though she has assiduously cultivated 'delicacy' in her charge, to hesitate about selling her child into a gross and destructive situation. In Mr. Mitchett she thinks she has found a desirable partner who will at once give Little Aggie marriage and protection." Mrs. Brook's daughter proposes to Mitchy to marry the girl, to save her from this contingency. And, seeing Nanda won't have him, he obligingly does.

Mrs. Brook is thus faced with a new situation upon which to employ her shrewd calculating faculty. When she obtains reason to feel that the old gentleman's affection for the young lady is such as to assure his money without the original marriage condition she discredits her daughter in the eyes of Vanderbank, and at the same time persuades Mr. Longdon to adopt her. This latter is arranged by making herself and her set so odious as to leave him no decent alternative but rescue the girl from their corrupting influence. Unfortunately, though, she overreaches herself in odiousness and disaffects the whole parcel of her cultivated friends (Van, Mitchy, the Duchess, etc.), thus breaking up her salon. It is up to Nanda then to try to rehabilitate her mother socially, and she does her best to achieve this by talking to Mitchy and Vanderbank before she goes off with Mr. Longdon.

"Ten long books to resolve so inconclusively, but so amusingly, the problem of getting a girl married," observed one commentator. "Van keeps himself free from marriage," another explained, "because he fears that marriage, a vested interest, would inevitably modify the range of his thought and the candor of his perception." "We are inclined," still another felt, "to set him down as an amiable philanderer, but James works hard to account for his supineness on other grounds. He implies in him enough affection to bring him repeatedly to the brink of a proposal, but checks him on each occasion by imputing to him a fastidiousness which proceeds, the reader suspects, rather from the lukewarmness of his passion than from the native fineness of his mind." "It is a tragedy of manners," another judged, "in which no genuine moral issue is involved, but in which vague depths of moral ugliness, especially in Vanderbank, are elusively but unforgettably suggested." Mrs. Brook, another has commented, "belongs with the charming rogues of literature, those characters whose energy redeems their badness and who, consequently, have no place in his regular scheme. It is she, the genius of conversation, who presides over the social entity in *The Awkward Age* and gives the novel its gravely festal air of having been written by someone on a dignified moral spree." "In the case of Mr. Longdon," another wrote, "the final result of his understanding was a shouldering of personal responsibility in the excellent tradition of his generation and according to the promptings of his own conscience and taste."

THE REAL STORY

The acts (or books) are ten in number, each a selected social occasion in the history and intercourse of the persons concerned, each marking a distinct phase in the development of the crisis, with an individual interest or character of its own, while still leading forward to the next. Each occasion as it advances the plot also exhibits one of the performers in especial, who lends that book his name; and as these divisions succeed one another the spotlight of interest shifts from character to character, arriving in the end at the young lady herself. That is to say, the subject is Nanda's predicament and the *dramatis personae* function actively only insofar as they are illuminational of that; but it is Mrs. Brook, Mr. Longdon, Van, Mitchy, and the others, with their own individual circumstances and states of mind, who make up the girl's affair for her, each of them constituting one part or aspect of it, and the sum of them, taken with her own attitude and her attributes, lighting up the subject on all of its sides.

The occasion of Book One is the first encounter of Mr. Longdon and Vanderbank, at the beginning of the season, shortly before Easter. They have met at Mrs. Brook's dinner-party and go to Van's rooms, there to draw each other out for the profit of the reader who in a preliminary way thus learns what he needs to know about the two men and about the affairs of the Brookenham household.

Mr. Longdon is an old man from the provinces who has been out of London thirty years, now come back, at a proper pitch of antiquity (he will never again see fifty-five, which was James's age when he wrote the work), full of the tone of time, to constitute as complete a case as possible of the sort of thing that will make him an anomaly and an outsider to the world of Buckingham Crescent, the social set, of the intensest modernity, presided over by Mrs. Brookenham, and of which Vanderbank is the chief ornament. Van is thirty-four and deputy chairman of the General Audit, a civil service position. Brookenham's place is also an "awfully good" one (his wife got it for him), Rivers and Lakes, but it's scarcely a sufficient basis in its pecuniarily picking-up character for the social status they attempt to build on it. He has, however, other moderate means, and to bolster their lively shakiness of fortune Mrs. Brook also must have had something in addition to her cleverness. They are "blessed

with" two grown children, Harold and Nanda, as well as
two small. Van goes to Buckingham Crescent every Sunday.
He has known Mrs. Brook for ten years: "But awfully well."

Mr. Longdon is an old boy who remembers the mothers—
Van's mother, distinctly, who had been kind to him—and
such a lot of Van's people. He most naturally tells the young
fellow of what happened in the antediluvian time, and in
particular about Mrs. Brook's mother, Lady Julia, with
whom he was very much in love, but vainly, and whom he
never managed to get over. Our gentleman of sentiment and
virtue, a quaint relic of the past, retired then without marrying to Beccles, there to grow into an apparently very rich
old man with no natural heir. Now here he is back in the
wonderful world that he long ago cut so loose from, and at
the very moment his beloved Lady Julia's grandaughter's
situation really begins to show. Book One is titled "Lady
Julia" and we see in it two differently constituted characters
profitably in talk together, or in "action," and we begin to
descry others, of a remoter intensity, getting into motion,
even if a bit vaguely yet, for our further enrichment.

The second act is placed in Mrs. Brook's drawing room,
into which there is rather a parade of characters, all bringing
with them the social atmosphere of the Buckingham Crescent
coterie. The Duchess warns Mrs. Brook that if she persists
in her perverse rearing of her child, Nanda will discover
that she can't decently marry: she'll have acquired a reputation for being "fast." The story's later events, as she might say,
justify her. The Duchess is carefully bringing up her own
orphaned niece Agnesina in the fine old foreign way, with
the emphasis of her education placed on what she is *not* to
learn—until the proper time. The Duchess introduces to the
drawing room her charming child, whose act it is, a pictured
and presented state of conformity, of disciplined submission,
of interested calculation, of emphasized virginity.

Mitchy is in the drawing room with his friend Lord
Petherton, with whom the Duchess has a clandestine relation.
Mitchy, Petherton, and the Duchess go off in a corner to
talk and Mrs. Brook converses with Mrs. Donner, a minor
character who has more recently entered. In the corner,

Petherton relates the anecdote of Carrie Donner's situation. Mr. Cashmore, it appears, Petherton's brother-in-law, who is "such a fine old ass," is "too thick with" Mrs. Donner, giving thereby his sister Fanny, Cashmore's wife, her "stupid grievance." The beauty of it, however, is that the two women seem never to let this interfere with their wonderful friendship. Mrs. Brook takes a great interest in marital difficulties and her information in this case regarding "the exact shade of the intimacy" between Mrs. Donner and Cashmore comes from none other than Nanda, who in turn gets it from Mrs. Donner's sister Tishy Grendon, a young unhappily married woman with whom the girl is great friends and "whose conversation has absolutely no limits." The moral for the Duchess is in what this particular friendship does to Nanda's innocence, which indeed is but one case of the general exposure to all sorts of undesirable information that any acquaintance between young unmarried and young married females is likely to entail. Nanda's view, incidentally, is that the accused Mr. Cashmore is in reality an innocent man.

Nanda has been talked about for two books, and in the Third her personal acquaintance is made, in Van's rooms, after the Easter holiday, by Mr. Longdon. Mitchy is there too, and Mrs. Brook had been invited but chose to send the girl alone to the three gentlemen. Her appearance makes its impression. Little Aggie's beauty is not of the glaring blatant bill-poster sort but Nanda's is still more obscure— though not altogether the puzzle perhaps that her mother seems to make it, and not at all to Mr. Longdon whose standards of it are from a different period of history. It is much rather Mrs. Brookenham's appearance that is in question for this gentleman; unless, indeed, she is to him as plain as possible. Mrs. Brook is so enormously different in every way from her mother, but Nanda's face isn't a bit modern. It's a face of Sir Thomas Lawrence or of Gainsborough. It's, Mr. Longdon assures us, Lady Julia in youth resurrected.

It's *she* again, as I first knew her, to the life; and not only in feature, in stature, in color, in movement, but in every bodily mark and sign, in every look of the eyes, above all

—oh, to a degree!—in the sound, in the charm of the voice. She's *all* Lady Julia. There isn't a touch of her mother. It's unique—an absolute revival. I see nothing of her father, either—I see nothing of anyone else. Isn't it thought wonderful by everyone?

The resemblance moves him to tears. And the young lady's sensibility is enough, despite her upbringing, not to cynically take this show of emotion for something ridiculous or illustrative of quaintness, but meets it rather with some tears of her own. Mr. Longdon, in effect, transfers the Lady Julia sentiment to Nanda, and she gracefully accepts it. The tie thus formed stands behind and under everything that takes place between them from this point. The old gentleman is genuinely romantic—deeply, and perhaps for some readers foolishly, so. Book Three belongs of course to him.

Whenever Nanda, throughout the play, speaks to Mr. Longdon she tries to refrain from making allusions he won't like; tries to tone down her conversation. But she keeps forgetting.

NANDA: My grandmother must have been awfully nice, and I somehow don't see myself at all as the same sort of person.

MR. LONGDON: Oh, I don't say you're in the least the same sort: all I allude to is the miracle of the physical heredity. Nothing could be less like her than your manner and your talk.

Liking Nanda is a painful, gradual process for Mr. Longdon but he does the girl the justice to admit that, rightly considered, she isn't on this score blameable at all really: it's the consequence, as Nanda's brother puts it, of "our having to go on, by no fault of our own, as our parents start us." Nanda is the creature of her mother's system just as Aggie is the victim of the Duchess'. We're all "partly the result of other people," and Mr. Longdon comes to attribute to Mrs. Brook's inferior virtue and nefarious training whatever is different from Lady Julia in Nanda.

The Fourth Book is Mr. Cashmore's, who presents himself in Mrs. Brook's drawing room, ostensibly to discuss with her the troubles he has knotted himself into, but actually cherishing the hope that Nanda will come in. He's "horribly rich," "massive without majesty," a member of Commons, and "would have been very red-headed if he had not been very bald." He has been meeting Nanda at Tishy's, Mrs. Brook explains to Van, "and she has talked to him so effectually about his behavior that she has quite made him cease to think about Carrie. He prefers *her* now—and of course she's much nicer . . . She makes him feel so innocent and good." The young lady doesn't make an entry but instead sends a wire: "Tishy keeps me dinner and opera; clothes all right; return uncertain but if before morning have latchkey."

For the Fifth Book the background is a country house rented for the occasion by Mitchy, and the time is a weekend of late July. There are several scenes, mostly between two persons with an occasional overlapping of a third. On a Saturday afternoon, alone together in the garden, Van chats with Nanda amiably but without special affection. When she talks to Mr. Longdon immediately after, on the same spot, the girl nevertheless lets him know her opinion that Mitchy, impossible for herself, is a proper mate for Aggie.

The next afternoon the Duchess, after whom this book is titled, makes her opportunity to grab at the old gentleman on the terrace, and she finds him accessible to what she has to say. This of course is that Nanda should marry the very first moment: the entourage and the atmosphere of talk in which she has been steeped is, for a single girl, appalling. To make a sure thing of it Mr. Longdon "can *doter* the bride." He "can settle on her something that will make her a *parti*."

Nanda's own activity is toward stopping off, for herself, every question of anyone but Van. "If she wants me to succeed in arranging with Mr. Mitchett, can you ask," the Duchess inquires, "for a plainer sign of her private predicament?" Van, she is sure,

> has no means of his own at all, and if he doesn't believe in impecunious marriages it's not I who shall be shocked

at him. For myself, I simply despise them. He has nothing but a poor official salary. If it's enough for one, it would be little for two, and would be still less for half a dozen. They're just the people to have, that blessed pair, a fine old English family.

Mr. Longdon, however, has not been ignorant that Mrs. Brook favors Mr. Mitchett for her daughter. Because, the Duchess elucidates, "she wants 'old Van' herself."

I've seen perfectly from the first (*little Aggie's aunt reasons*) that the only difficulty would come from her mother—but also that that would be stiff.

The Duchess does interest Mr. Longdon and moves him. She gives the old gentleman in a full and lucid way what he had already taken in from various signs, and she helps him to his solution. She brings him to the point at which all that he sees and feels and puts together in this connection eventuates in a decision which he communicates to Van, as their relations permit, late that night, alone together in the billiards room of Mertle. The previous business of the act has all been preparation for this.

Mr. Longdon, in short, wants Nanda to marry to such a tune "that on the day she does she'll come into the interest of a considerable sum of money" he has determined to settle upon her. He is prepared to be more explicit but Van sees that the awkwardness will be minimized for himself if his elderly friend doesn't exactly express, or anything like it, what the money is. At any rate, and as a matter of some urgency, Mr. Longdon wants her "got out."

VAN: "Out"?
MR. LONGDON: Out of her mother's house.
VAN: Why, her mother's house is just where I see her!
MR. LONGDON: Precisely; and if it only were not, we might get on faster.

Mr. Longdon shows himself here in agreement with the Duchess: that Mrs. Brook's house is one of corruption for young girls and that the woman will move strenuously to block the marriage of her daughter to this charming young man.

MR. LONGDON: I'm thinking of what the meaning is of Mrs. Brookenham's wanting you—as I've heard it called—herself.

VAN (*still with his smile, smoking a minute*): That's what you've heard it called?

MR. LONGDON: Yes, but you must excuse me from telling you by whom.

VAN: It's unimaginable. But it doesn't matter. We all call everything—anything. The meaning of it, if you and I put it so, is—well, a modern shade.

MR. LONGDON: You must deal then yourself with your modern shades.

All of Nanda's mother's relation with Vanderbank that is of the subject is given by dramatic projection, as all the rest is given, and if it is "an alliance it would have been difficult to explain at Beccles" we needn't jump to conclusions from that.

The situation belongs, I think, to an order I don't understand (*the Duchess confesses to Mr. Longdon*). I understand either one thing or the other—I understand taking a man up or letting him alone. But I don't, really, get at Mrs. Brook. You must judge, at any rate, for yourself.

Judgment will depend on the reader's general vision of things and his sense of signs. We are at liberty to infer a relation other than friendship if that's the way the characters in question strike us; and appearances, as interpreted by ourselves, may seem strongly to back us up. However, none of them will be of a *determinant* character, while on the contrary side flourish significations that are really conclusive. The conviction of many readers will remain unshaken on this point, however: so great is James's skill at planting illusory indications to raise certain suspicions and then developing them to resemble almost indistinguishably the true.

> Supply any sense whatever that may miraculously satisfy your fond English imagination (*the Duchess permits Mr. Longdon*). I don't insist in the least on a bad one. She does want him for herself—that's all I say.

There are people in the play to tell the reader and each other that Mrs. Brook wants Van for herself, it being so the circle of talk, reference, gossip; but we may have our own estimate of the truth of ever so much chatter in general, and of that chatter in particular. We take the relation as treated to be a representative sample of the wonderful air James has of inviting competitive suggestions. And from the play of such oppositions, of course, arises the author's famed ambiguity. Some readers may discover a charm, as he did, "in any produced ambiguity of appearance that is not by the same stroke, and all helplessly, an ambiguity of sense."

But no more evidence is needed to convince us of the reality of Nanda's crush on Van. Nothing has come of it because, although he has been aware and has been nice and kind to her, he isn't affected in the same way; is in these matters too cool and calculating a bird. He likes women, yes; and has had lots to do with them; but in the way of what a real relation with *her* would mean—not! He has thought her rather nice but hasn't really at all *cared* for her, keeping himself in reserve as it is of his essence to do. Then, too, she is fourteen years the younger and still an adolescent. He feels a delicacy. "He wants not to be an ass on the one side, and yet not some other kind of brute on the other." He wants not, equally, to close altogether, by a promptly negative word, the question of his marrying money —if he gets something *more* than merely that. That isn't the form that his delicacy takes. She does have a kind of attraction for him, and he hasn't ever considered or observed her with any such possibility in mind. So we see the young man, with the recognition of what it involves for him, asking for time, which Mr. Longdon is obliged to grant.

MR. LONGDON (*pulling out his watch*): It's one o'clock.

VAN: Oh, I require more than tonight!

Mr. Longdon tells him that he must take of course the time he needs. The story, on these lines, has been set up in the first half of the play for working out in the second; and in the interest of balance and proportion the two "halves" are equal in length without crowding of one to make them so.

Van feels he can't arrive at any attitude in the matter without taking Mrs. Brook into his confidence, and the occasion on which he does this, in her drawing room, three days after the Sunday spent at Mertle, gives us the woman drawn out in a way that is surely a contribution to the subject and makes the aspect, Book Six, her own. Mitchy drops in on the two and she immediately imparts to him the news of dear Mr. Longdon's "wish to make it worth somebody's while to marry my child."

MITCHY: "Make it"? But *isn't* it?

MRS. BROOK: My dear friend, you must ask Van. Of course you've always thought so. But I must tell you, all the same, that I'm delighted.

Nanda's mother admits the interest of the case. Only, to be perfect, it lacks the element of real suspense—or so she thinks:

He'll be charming, touching, confiding—above all he'll be awfully *interesting* about it. But he'll make up his mind in his own way, and his own way won't be to accommodate Mr. Longdon.

Nor is there anything to definitely indicate that Mrs. Brook is not here, with a sincerity and frankness that is not feigned or simulated, offering Van the truth, as she sees it, about himself. The question of whether or no he shall becomes *the* question; just as the way he answers it, not all at once but under further impressions evoked, becomes a thing of the liveliest interest for us.

What is fine in the talk the three of them have together—an informal meeting of the inner circle of Buckingham Crescent

—is the freedom and good humor and intelligence of their intercourse. They do care to get at the ideas of things, as Van says: "to take in the truth of the case and make the best of that." Nonetheless, the relations of the characters being what they are, this question hanging now in the balance touches all of them, those present in this scene and those not, and has the effect of introducing a latent tension or suspense when almost any two of them come together; a quiet tenseness and curiosity not at all detrimental to the dramatic quality of their conversations. What stupefies Van somewhat "is the extraordinary critical freedom—or we may call it if we like the high intellectual detachment—with which we discuss a question touching you, dear Mrs. Brook, so nearly and engaging so your private and sacred sentiments. What are we playing with, after all, but the idea of Nanda's happiness?"

MRS. BROOK: Oh, I'm not playing!

MITCHY: She's not playing. Don't you feel in the very air the vibration of the passion that she's simply too charming to shake at the window as the housemaid shakes the table-cloth or the jingo the flag?

Half an hour after Mrs. Brook's visitors depart, Nanda enters to find her mother still on the sofa in the drawing room. The girl was first introduced as a matter of her relation with Mr. Longdon, lighting up *their* situation; but now she is "with" her mother, and it is the domestic situation of the Brookenhams that we are treated to, especial reference being placed on Nanda's part in it from her mother's point of view. Mr. Longdon figures here only as he may be connected with that. They are a relatively poor family in a society of rich, living to some extent on their bounty; predatory on the very rich for hospitalities. To hold on takes them to the very brink of their means, and before them is always an abyss of inconvenience, an abyss of inability to keep it up combined with the social impossibility of not doing so. Mrs. Brook has got quarters lent her for the two small children and their people at Bognor. Harold is to be off somewhere visiting. And the husband and wife have a very full schedule of places. Nanda's invitation is from Mr. Longdon:

MR. LONGDON: But come down to Suffolk for sanity . . . I want to show you what life *can* give. Not, of course, of this sort of thing.

NANDA: No—you've told me. Of peace.

Her mother inquires of Nanda whether the girl is not bored by long hours spent with a "fussy, ancient man": a man who describes himself as "no talker myself. I'm old-fashioned and narrow and dull. I've lived for years in a hole. I'm not a man of the world." What is her daughter to gain in exchanging the great world of Buckingham Crescent society for the little world of Beccles? The young lady expresses her pleasure just in being liked so much. Mr. Longdon goes home on Saturday, and if it suits her mother's arrangements she may accompany him down on the train, for a visit without any calculated end.

MRS. BROOK: What do you call that then but his adopting you?

NANDA: Ah, I don't know that it matters much what it's called.

MRS. BROOK: So long as it brings with it, you mean, all the advantages?

NANDA: Well yes, call them advantages.

MRS. BROOK: One would be quite ready to do that if one only knew a little more exactly what you're to get by them.

NANDA: Oh, the great advantage, I feel, is doing something for *him*.

MRS. BROOK: But doesn't that, my dear, put the extravagance of your surrender to him on rather an odd footing? Charity, love, begins at home, and if it's a question of merely *giving*, you've objects enough for your bounty without going so far.

NANDA: Why, I thought you wanted me so to be nice to him!

MRS. BROOK: Well, I hope you won't think me very vulgar

if I tell you that I want you still more to have some idea of what you'll get by it. I've no wish to keep on boring you with Mitchy—

NANDA: Don't, don't!

MRS. BROOK: Then what do you get instead?

NANDA: Instead of Mitchy? Oh, I shall never marry.

MRS. BROOK: Well then, we shall consider—your father and I—that he must take the consequence.

NANDA: "He"?

MRS. BROOK: I mean Mr. Longdon.

NANDA: And what do you mean by the consequence?

MRS. BROOK: Well, it will do for the beginning of it that you'll please go down *with* him.

NANDA: On Saturday then? Thanks, mamma.

The next step in the drama occurs three weeks later at Mr. Longdon's charming old place in Suffolk. The persons involved are Nanda, Mitchy, and Van—the last two down only for the weekend. The first scene is between Nanda and Van: the passage *after* the blessed man's generous bribe, which is a pendant to the passage before. Like the other, this scene is set in a garden, a propitious quiet resort for a proposal. But our young man, as yet uncertain, his mind not yet made up, forbears, abstains, shows himself still "in suspense about himself." What he says to Nanda is in the way, largely, of *not* saying.

The next afternoon, in Mr. Longdon's drawing room, Nanda points out to Mitchy the beauty of his chance to save the young Agnesina from her alleged protector.

NANDA: Keep her from becoming like the Duchess.

MITCHY: But she isn't a bit like the Duchess in any of her elements. She's a totally different thing.

NANDA: That's exactly why she'll be so perfect for you. You'll get her away—take her out of her aunt's life.

It also, in a manner, disposes of *him*—so that if the other young man, the one of social charm and striking good looks, should have in mind to propose to herself he won't be hindered, as he at present may be, since he still rather strangely stands off, over scruples, over worries about cutting across the possibility of a friend, over depriving her of something in the shape of a man with Mitchy's amount of money that she may live to regret and languish for.

Mitchy agrees. He does it frankly to oblige; yet keeping his head, as it were, and deciding quite on his own grounds. He's clever, as Van and the Duchess and of course Mrs. Brook are clever—it's a circle of clever people, but the note we know him by, the deep thing in him, is his infatuation with Mrs. Brookenham's daughter; just as the special sign of Nanda is her terrific crush on Van; or, of Mr. Longdon, the Lady Julia sentiment. This principal motive force annihilates or directs all those which, had he been another man in such a situation, would normally come into play.

In a letter to Henrietta Reubell, James summarized the state of mind imputable:

> It's absolute to him that Nanda will never have him—and she *appeals* to him for another girl, whom she sees him as "saving" (from things—realities she sees). If he does it (and she shows how she values him by wanting it) it is still a way of getting and keeping near her—of making for *her*, to him, a tie of gratitude. She becomes, as it were, to him, responsible for his happiness—they can't (*especially if the marriage goes ill*) *not* be—given the girl that Nanda is—more, rather than less, together. And the finale of the picture *justifies* him: it leaves Nanda, precisely, with his case on her hands. Farfetched? Well, I daresay: but so are diamonds and pearls and the beautiful Reubell turquoises!

The fellow isn't right for Aggie, obviously, since he doesn't love her. He undertakes the marriage with the idea of making the relation between himslf and his wife part and parcel of his relation with Nanda. It is positively in his interest, as he sees it for himself, that his marriage should go badly—because that will bring him closer to Nanda.

For the final scene under Mr. Longdon's roof, in the August night, with the lamp extinguished to favor talk, Van and Mitchy discuss the latter's decision to apply to the Duchess for her niece. This Book highlights the situation of Mitchy, and is titled accordingly, as it contributes its due share to the picture of Nanda Brookenham's situation. What the fellow announces his intention of undertaking, in its immediate appearance, adds his name to the list of those who have done what they are able, each in his own way, to try to bring Vanderbank to the point with Nanda.

VAN: Do you like so very much little Aggie?
MITCHY: Well, Nanda does. And I like Nanda.
VAN: You're too amazing. I can't help its coming over me then that, on such an extraordinary system, you must also rather like *me*.

Van, Mitchy reminds him, is of a special class: one of those who are "a source of the sacred terror. People made in such a way must take the consequences; just as people must take them who are made as I am. So cheer up!" "Happy relations don't matter," Nanda explains to Van. "I always think of you with fear." The loved object is a source of terror to the lover. In *The Ambassadors* it is of Chadwick Newsome that Madame de Vionnet is afraid. And fear of losing *his* precious creature altogether, not the mere liking of Van, impels Mitchy to take the awful step.

Mitchy produces his impression that Nanda has her idea, from having guessed, of Mr. Longdon's readiness to settle—providing the so beastly good-looking, intelligent, and amiable young fellow consents to do the rest. Van feels this for himself: "If only because she knows everything. She knows everything, everything."

MITCHY: Everything, everything.
VAN: She told me so herself yesterday.
MITCHY: And she told *me* so today.

Whereas a young lady bred as the Duchess breeds little Aggie knows little or nothing about the world. Knowing everything is an attitude perhaps not inconsistent with adolescence, when a good deal that has been found out is still fresh in the mind. At any rate, Nanda's whole conduct is an expression of that belief. Intelligence, character, sense of life and knowledge of it, however, imply a certain experience and a certain time for that.

The Duchess succeeded in marrying Aggie to the very fellow Mrs. Brook wanted for Nanda and had been urging on Nanda. The Continental plan, we can imagine the woman to feel, has had its superiority dramatically illuminated: a social scheme that absolutely prevents awkwardness, as contrasted with something morally well-meant but intellectually helpless. The system of free choice has suffered its victim to be left in question. For when Book Eight opens it is ten weeks after Mitchy's wedding, six months since Mr. Longdon's proposal of a definite basis, and Vanderbank hasn't yet done it, neither one way nor the other. The standing off from sharp or supreme clearances confirms itself as being a note of his action in the matter. Nanda, for her part, continues to hope; and the Duchess descends again upon Mr. Longdon.

All of the characters are in the Eighth Book, on a January evening, at a going-away party for Aggie and Mitchy held in young Mrs. Grendon's drawing room, a circumstance that gives this division its title. Tishy Grendon is "bodily speaking a beautiful human plant." As for cleverness, she admits to understanding the Buckingham Crescent people only "when Nanda explains. In fact there's scarcely anything I understand except when Nanda explains. It's too dreadful her being away so much now with strange people, whom I'm sure she can't begin to do for what she does for me." Nanda has been, all the intervening five months, with Mr. Longdon at Beccles. In the first scene Vanderbank, upon arriving early, talks to the girl.

VAN: Jolly, at any rate, thanks to my mistake, to have in this way a quiet moment with you. You came on ahead of your mother?

NANDA: Oh no—I'm staying here.

VAN: Oh!

NANDA: Mr. Longdon came up with me—I came here, Friday last, straight.

VAN: You parted at the door?

NANDA: Yes—but only for a day or two. He's coming tonight.

Her living with these other people so much, Mr. Longdon and Tishy, although her parents are about is symptomatic of a note deep in the girl. The relation of Nanda to her mother is sufficiently there, but—according to James's method—only as an implied and indicated thing. The relation of Mr. Longdon to Mrs. Brook is founded on the unconscious violence offered by both her nature and her appearance to every memory of Lady Julia. He quite detests her. He wants to save the child from her. Nanda's attitude, normal to adolescence, is perfectly in line with this low opinion of her parents. *Her* imagination also is engaged in the task of getting free of them.

This step in development (*Freud writes*) is not merely a question of a change of object. The turning away from the mother occurs in an atmosphere of antagonism; the attachment to the mother ends in hate. Such a hatred may be very marked and may persist throughout an entire lifetime; it may later on be carefully overcompensated; as a rule, one part of it is overcome, while another part persists.

In this case, the relation of her mother to Van would only aggravate the girl's emotion. That there is a liking in the other direction, from the young man to her mother, is something she can't bring herself to admit. But Van's high regard for Mrs. Brook keeps coming out all through the play.

The Duchess asks Mr. Longdon to please remember that Mrs. Brook, from her own point of view, has her grievance. She has, in a manner of speaking, "put down her money without a return. She has given Mitchy up and got nothing instead." There's therefore, in the state of mind the Duchess attributes to Mrs. Brook, a danger to the idea of marrying the girl to Van.

Just in her feeling, in the case, as most women would feel. You see she did what she could for her daughter. She did, I'm bound to say, as that sort of thing goes among you people, a good deal. She treasured up, she nursed along Mitchy, whom she would also, though of course not so much, have liked for herself. Nanda, with a word, could have kept him on, becoming thereby, for *your* plan, so much the less accessible.

The Duchess's aspect, however, in this Book isn't altogether without competition, for Mrs. Brook is now in the field; and, prompted by another connection, has an edifying word to say about grievances:

MRS. BROOK: The beauty of the life that so many of us have so long led together is precisely that nobody has ever had one. Nobody has dreamed of it—it would have been such a rough, false note, a note of violence out of all keeping. Did you ever hear of one, Van? Did you, my poor Mitchy? But you see for yourselves how inferior we've become when we have even in our defense to assert such things.

At any rate, the Duchess holds to her original opinion.

DUCHESS: She wants him herself.
MR. LONGDON: And he doesn't—not a bit—want *her!*
DUCHESS: It's really only for Nanda he cares.
MR. LONGDON: Yes—really.
DUCHESS: And yet exactly how much?
MR. LONGDON: I haven't asked him.
DUCHESS: Don't you think it about time you *should?*

Mr. Longdon, for reasons, never inquires. But Mrs. Brook goes into action.

MR. LONGDON: What, after all, can she do?
DUCHESS: She can *keep* Mr. Van.
MR. LONGDON: Where?
DUCHESS: I mean till it's too late. She can work on him.

MR. LONGDON: But how?
DUCHESS: Sit down—you'll see.

Mr. Longdon does "see" after this giving away of Mrs. Brook
by the Duchess in the sense of fixing her forthcoming behavior upon the old gentleman, or inviting him to fix it:
showing him, in advance, a light on how to take it.

What Mrs. Brook does isn't very violent, although everything precedent has been preparation for this climactic scene,
so that the whole effect has been gathered there ready to
break. Nanda's mother merely conditions its breaking to in-
sure that it does so in the right way. Accompanied by Van,
she comes over to Mr. Longdon and the Duchess for a chat.
The four are gradually joined by the others to compose
a pleasant talkative ring; one in which, with Mrs. Brook
directing the conversation, the spirit of gossip governs. After
letting the gentleman from Beccles observe the kind of morals
and manners and talk to be had in present-day good society,
and indeed making him the butt of some of it, Nanda's
mother further uses the occasion to tell him, in the presence
of them all, that she wants her child back, as a felt domestic
need.

Then there is the little business of the French novel, a
thing in blue paper lent Mrs. Brook by Van months ago,
which she uses to bring Book Eight to its close. Aggie, who
since her marriage has "come out" with a bound, found it
lying about on one of Mrs. Grendon's tables as a stage property, with Van's name written on the cover. Petherton, in
sport, wrested it from Mitchy's wife "to see if it's good for
her." Mrs. Brook notices that the writing isn't Van's hand,
and points this out to Mr. Longdon. Nanda is forced to
explain.

NANDA: It was I who wrote Mr. Van's name. I brought
the book here from Buckingham Crescent and left it by
accident in the other room.
MRS. BROOK: By accident, my dear, I do quite hope. But
what on earth did you bring it for? It's too hideous.
NANDA: Is it?

MRS. BROOK: Then you haven't read it?
NANDA: One hardly knows now, I think, what is and what isn't.

The person upon whom Mr. Longdon will work off his distaste for the ugliness of the child's having read an indecent French novel is suggested in Nanda's reply. Raised in the *mal aria* these people have made for her, how, really, could a girl be expected to know better? It furnishes the last proof, were one needed for this gentleman, of the necessity of her removal. Mrs. Brook does not give up the point of her amiable inquiry. She presses her daughter to bring straight out what she had not yet succeeded in saying with sufficient plainness.

MRS BROOK: Have you read this work, Nanda?
NANDA: Yes, mamma.
MR. CASHMORE (*hilarious and turning the leaves*): Oh, I say!
MR. LONGDON (*ceremoniously approaching Tishy*): Good night.

Mr. Longdon would be quite at one with the Duchess as to the reason for Mrs. Brook's making it a matter of such importance the company should know her daughter had read the horrid work. They would see the woman as wishing to discredit her daughter's innocence in the wavering mind of Vanderbank, hoping thereby to degrade her in his eyes and cause him to throw her over. But a belief in Mrs. Brook's character requires us to look for a different interpretation. Mrs. Brook is aware of the confidence now ruling the relation between Mr. Longdon and Nanda. Nothing *she* in particular can do or say will shake that. And what makes it really certain to her that the old gentleman will stick is just that the young gentleman hasn't. Mr. Longdon would read Van's abandoning of the girl to be the result of Mrs. Brook's machinations of exposure, and this would make the child's case all the more compassionate to him. It would also point up the urgency of the antidote: A continuation of the dose of the

purer air of Suffolk, a place where she at least may breathe.
And we see Mrs. Brook concurring that for Nanda, now
everything else has failed, there is nothing but Mr. Longdon.
Mitchy is married, and as for the Van affair being off—when
was it on?

In words quoted previously, the Duchess alludes to Mr.
Longdon's plan. If Nanda had kept Mitchy on, this would
have resulted in the girl's "becoming thereby, for *your* plan,
so much the less accessible."

MR. LONGDON: What do you know of my "plan"?
DUCHESS: Why, my dear man, haven't I told you that ever
since Mertle, I've made out your hand? What on earth,
for other people, can your action look like but an adoption?
MR. LONGDON: Of—a—*him?*
DUCHESS: You're delightful. Of—a—*her!* If it comes to
the same thing for you, so much the better. That, at any
rate is what we're all taking it for, and Mrs. Brook herself
en tête. She sees—through your generosity—Nanda's life,
more or less, at the worst, arranged for, and that's just what
gives her a good conscience.

That Nanda has been adopted is what neither the girl nor
the old gentleman will concede. She hasn't in any formal
and final sense left her parents and gone over to Mr. Longdon
with a definite understanding. She hasn't wanted Van to
suppose or be sure that she *can.* The young man, she realizes,
doesn't want her through his action to miss a fortune. "I want
so awfully to be kind to her," he says to Mitchy on one
occasion.

The explanation, then, of his delay in reporting back to
Mr. Longdon his decision, if we are so kind as not to attribute
to him a disreputable motive, is that he has been watching for
some sign of this of a nature that will eliminate all doubt,
and that this is precisely what the girl, Mr. Longdon aiding,
is determined not to let him have. Nanda wishes him to believe that her enjoyment of Mr. Longdon's money is staked
on his action, not that she'll get it, or a provision of it,
whatever happens. The *impasse* thus created constitutes the

nature of the crisis to which Mrs. Brook's intervention will bring relief. The woman, by "calling in" her daughter, is applying pressure upon the girl to decide. She has either to come back in obedience to her mother's public request to Mr. Longdon or else let herself be adopted immediately. But if she returns to her mother's house, then it is Mr. Longdon who will apply pressure for the adoption. From the point of view of "Beccles," Buckingham Crescent is a place of horrors, and Nanda, for being raised in its immoral atmosphere, an object deserving of pity. Mr. Longdon sees for himself, and Mrs. Brook has helped him see, the infections caught by the girl from the behavior of those about her. And to help Nanda's mother produce the desired bad impression on Mr. Longdon, at Mrs. Grendon's and elsewhere, everyone works together, all instinctively and unconsciously. Harold assists immensely; Mr. Brook not so much, but still he helps; the "outer circle" also who come to the house: Cashmore, Carrie, Tishy, Fanny—each in their degree. Nor do the Duchess and Petherton fail to contribute to this effect. The *ensemble* at Mrs. Grendon's, with all its accompanying aspects, "where," James pronounced in his preface, "the 'cross references' of the action are as thick as the green leaves of a garden, but none the less, as they have scenically to be, counted and disposed, weighted with responsibility," gathers the action up to the fullness desired and constitutes Book Eight, or Act Eight, of the drama, with the denouement occupying the space to the end, after which there are but two books left.

The Ninth Book, "Vanderbank," an afternoon late in May, restores us to the drawing room at Buckingham Crescent. The young man who gives his stamp to this occasion hasn't been in, except for a few times with other people, since the night of Tishy's dinner party in January. He turns up alone now and has a little talk with Mrs. Brook. Nanda has come back, and Mrs. Brook has placed at her disposal a sitting room and one of the men, in addition to her maid. In order to give Van more time we suppose that she has asked Mr. Longdon for a delay. But for a pointed indication to the girl of his lack of "intentions," yet diplomatic and indirect as is his fashion, the young man, since her return, has been keeping his beautiful presence away from the house.

MRS. BROOK: I sometimes think, in effect, that you're incapable of anything straightforward!
VAN: Don't you call it straightforward of me just not to have come for so long?

Mitchy and his wife have just returned from the Mediterranean, and the Duchess is in a state over the base defection of Petherton who was with the pair for weeks.

VAN: Do you mean then that he *is* such a brute that after all Mitchy has done for him—?
MRS. BROOK: I think him quite capable of considering, with a magnificent insolence of selfishness, that what Mitchy has *most* done will have been to make Aggie accessible in a way that—for decency and delicacy of course, things on which Petherton highly prides himself—she could naturally *not* be as a girl. Her marriage has simplified it.

Mrs. Brook is equally explanatory about Mitchy.

MRS. BROOK: He *may* not become unhappy—God grant *not!* But if he does he'll take it out of Nanda.
VAN: "Take it out" of her?
MRS. BROOK: Well, want to know, as some American asked me the other day of somebody, what she's "going to do" about it.
VAN: But what *can* she "do"—?
MRS. BROOK: That's again just what I'm curious to see.

Since the girl's return, Cashmore has been running in and out of the house without bothering to speak to Mrs. Brook, while Harold has been having some success at amusing his wife. Van, before going upstairs to see Nanda, asks:

VAN: I ask you what in the world—since Harold keeps Fanny so quiet—Cashmore requires Nanda's direction for?

MRS. BROOK: Ah, find out!

VAN: Isn't Carrie Donner quite shelved?

MRS. BROOK: Find out!

VAN: You scarce suppose, I imagine, that she has come to like him "for himself"?

Van has already applied to Nanda his measure of taste and delicacy and the sympathetic and the nice and the what he wants; now he weighs her action in the Cashmore and Mitchy affairs against his own sense of fineness in these matters. They reinforce his vision of how she is. This act of seeing in itself is not pictured, but his decision is the dramatic assurance or demonstration of it.

The second scene is between Mrs. Brook and her husband after Van has left without going up to Nanda. Upon second thoughts, he couldn't risk not giving her this additional hint. The third is between Mrs. Brook and Mitchy. Upon his return from abroad he has come to call. Mr. Longdon is also arriving and Mrs. Brook arranges for him to receive a piece of news from a source more believable than herself. She requests Mitchy to put before the old gentleman what has "happened here today. Van's marked retreat, and how, with the time that has passed, it makes us at last know where we are. You of course, for yourself, see that." Mitchy duly carries out the errand.

MITCHY: Well, he was, after a long absence, here a while since, as if expressly to see her. But after spending half an hour, he went away without it.

MR. LONGDON: He spent the half-hour with her mother instead?

Mr. Longdon would know in what light to regard this fact. Van, having finally made up his mind to propose, and calling for the purpose, was put off again by some supreme trick that Mrs. Brook has played upon her daughter.

Nanda holds the stage throughout the three scenes of the concluding book, in her upstairs sitting room, in talks with Van, Mitchy, and finally Mr. Longdon, a fortnight after the old gentleman's return. Van's appointment is first; he has come in response to her note. Mr. Longdon, we infer, is in town to obtain either Nanda or her refusal, and the girl has sent for the young man simply to take a last look at him before going away. But she has of course a different reason prepared. It pleases her to interpret Van's non-calling as motivated by his disgust of Mrs. Brook, and the young lady arrives at an uplifted view of her opportunity to rectify this.

NANDA: She has more or less—by his marriage—lost Mitchy. I don't want her to lose everything. Do stick to her . . . I suppose it *would* be immodest if I were to say that I verily believe she's in love with you. Not, for that matter, that father would mind—he wouldn't mind, as he says, a two-penny rap. . . . When I think of her downstairs there so often nowadays practically alone, I feel as if I could scarcely bear it. She's so fearfully young.

Van promises her that these words have stayed him in his course.

VAN: You've made me stand as still as Joshua made the sun. "Young," you say she is? It's not like anything else. She's youth. She's *my* youth—she *was* mine. And if you ever have a chance do put in for me that, if she wants *really* to know, she's booked for my old age. She's clever enough, you know, to understand what you tell her.

NANDA: And then she's so lovely.

VAN: Awfully pretty!

NANDA: I don't say it; as they say, you know, *because* she's mother, but I often think when we're out that wherever she is—

VAN: There's no one that, all round, really touches her? Oh, so every one thinks, and in fact one's appreciation of the charming things that, in that way, are so intensely her own, can scarcely breathe on them all lightly enough. And then, hang it, she has perceptions—which are not things that run about the streets. She has surprises. She has little ways.

NANDA: Well, I'm glad you do like her.

VAN: I like, you know, about as well as I ever liked any-thing this wonderful idea of yours putting in a plea for her solitude and her youth. Don't think I do it injustice if I say—which is saying much—that it's quite as charming as it's amusing. And now good-by.

Mitchy, when he comes in, is informed of the success of the girl's appeal.

NANDA: He's going, all the same, Mr. Van, to be charming to mother. We've settled that.

And from the same sense of filial duty a supplication goes out to this young man also.

MITCHY: One simply *doesn't* give her up. One can't.

Moreover, Aggie is in Mrs. Brook's regular line.

MITCHY: Your mother will attract her, study her, finally "understand" her. In fact, she'll help her, as she has helped so many before, and will help so many still to come.

Aggie's husband will of course be Nanda's problem, whom she promises not to "abandon."

The girl on the morrow will go off with Mr. Longdon, but first, in the concluding scene, the pair discuss why it is that Van hasn't stuck. Their apprehension of the elements oper-ative for him throws light on both of the analysts, and parti-cularly on the girl, this being *her* aspect. Nanda's presence in the circle of free talk and manners at Buckingham Crescent has destroyed her innocence in the sense of initiating her into matters from which a girl should decently have been guarded. They see Van as horror-struck by the awful amount that the young lady has seen and knows.

NANDA: Everything's different from what it used to be.
MR. LONGDON: Yes, everything. That's what he ought to have recognized.

NANDA: As *you* have? Oh, he's more old-fashioned than you.

MR. LONGDON: Much more.

NANDA: He tried—he did his best. But he couldn't. And he's so right—for himself.

MR. LONGDON: He ought to have married—

NANDA: Little Aggie? Yes.

MR. LONGDON: And then Mitchy—

NANDA: No—not even then!

MR. LONGDON: Are you anxious about Mitchy?

NANDA: Yes. Do you see? There I am.

MR. LONGDON: I see. There we are. Well—tomorrow.

THE WINGS OF THE DOVE

THE ROMANCE

KATE CROY is engaged to wed Merton Densher but there is
the matter of money. The young woman lives with her
widowed aunt Mrs. Maud Lowder in her sumptuous London
home and on her freely given charity; while the young man
draws a salary from a newspaper office that is sufficient to
support no one but himself. Mrs. Lowder does not disapprove
of the fellow personally, simply on his want of means. She
has hopes of a better marriage for her niece who has beauty
and brains and social aplomb. It is not left obscure that only
for a marriage highly suitable would the wealthy relative
who has produced her in society furnish the proper dowry.
The most acceptable suitor within range is Lord Mark, a
nobleman of rather limited estate unluckily, and also a poor
creature in some other respects, but who does have a rank
that permits him to move in exclusive circles. Kate decides
to keep her betrothal secret and to wait.

This is the setting into which the orphan Milly Theale,
tragic and touching, brings from America to Landcaster Gate
her youth and innocence, her precarious health, and her
great monetary resources. Thanks to this combination, the
last item not counting the least, she rapidly becomes a tremendous success in the Lowder social set. Mrs. Lowder herself is pleased to regard the girl as a suitable match for Densher. Merton had known Milly in New York. She had been
kind to him during a reportorial assignment there and he
is pleased to renew the acquaintance. It soon becomes a
generally known, if not openly discussed, fact that Milly is
quite fond of the handsome young newspaperman; and Aunt
Maud, for points of view of her own, takes a personal interest

44

in doing what she can to further this affair. Milly, it may be remarked at this point, although only twenty-two is alone in Europe and in the world, having had the appalling misfortune to lose all of her relatives. She has merely her attendant friend Mrs. Susan Shepherd Stringham, a Bostonian widow in her middle years. Mrs. Stringham's loyalty to Milly however, it may suit the reader to know, appears to be quite selfless. And Mrs. Stringham's views coincide with Mrs. Lowder's as to the consideration Densher should bestow upon Milly.

Kate also enthusiastically agrees to do what she can to promote the wedding of Milly to the young man. She has concealed from Milly as well as from everyone else her betrothal to Densher and once Mrs. Lowder's coolly calculating niece perceives that the American girl is dying she urges upon her fiancé that here is his perfect chance to develop within a relatively short time into a very rich young widower.

Milly and Mrs. Stringham go on from London to Venice accompanied by Mrs. Lowder and Kate. Lord Mark and Densher arrive separately. Without loss of time the penniless peer proposes to the American girl and is with as little delay rejected. She lets him have as a reason his known prior interest in her good friend Kate; and when he surmises that Miss Croy is not really unattached Milly is able to contradict this from the best of sources.

Mrs. Lowder and Kate return to London after an interval, leaving Milly and Mrs. Stringham in a Venetian palazzo which the American girl has rented. But before Kate departs she arranges that Merton shall stay in Venice. Densher's resentment has not been severe while it remained a matter of merely philandering under orders with a thoroughly attractive girl but at this turn he threatens to rebel and is dissuaded only by the surrender Kate makes to him in his rooms.

Lord Mark back in London proposes now to Kate. Rebuffed again, in a flash of divination he seees the plot; and— for motives that are either moral or vindictive or mercenary —communicates what he suspects to Milly. The girl's will to live, which had been the chief factor keeping her alive, is broken by the shock of such news. Her health totally collapses and despite the ministrations of her London physician who hastens to Italy she soon dies. But as a sign of forgiveness and for a remembrance of her love she bequeaths her money to Densher. The generosity and death of the American girl produce their effect upon the young man. He becomes more thoroughly ashamed of his fiancée's idea, conceives an utter horror of it and of his part in it. In that horror he draws close to the dead girl. In the light of how exquisite the dead girl was he perceives how little exquisite is the living. He offers to complete his bargain with Kate but she sufficiently sees that he is now in love with Milly's memory and she gives him up. "One who was pure in heart had confounded them, the wicked and the weak," wrote one commentator. "Though death had come to Milly Theale it had not brought victory to the survivors, and Milly had left behind her one who would cherish her memory forever."

THE REAL STORY

Milly is a young woman gravely sick. There is a drama constituted by the conflict within herself, between her stricken state and her will to live, and tragedy in the defeat, ultimately, of the latter. There are also the things she founds her struggle on, the particular human interests she lives for, the people she becomes involved with. These people, to whom her condition is as the pool of a Lorelei, tempting or charming them from more prescribed orbits, are affected in ways that make them part of the action. Her struggle becomes their drama too. The center of interest is in Milly Theale's influence.

The loss of one's entire family in childhood and early youth—parents, brothers, sisters, cousins, aunts—might induce a state of grief and painful dejection amounting, in a person with any predisposition, to melancholy. But Milly puts on a brave front and is fiercely shy about so personal a secret as her illness. She is too proud for pity or even for tears. When she and Kate are thrown together in London the two quickly become friends and when the American girl pays her first visit to the eminent Harley Street specialist her English companion waits in the outer office.

SIR LUKE STRETT: Hard things have come to you in youth, but you mustn't think life will be for you all hard things. You've the right to be happy. You must make up your mind to it. You must accept any form in which happiness may come . . . You're active, luckily, by nature—it's beautiful: therefore rejoice in it. *Be* active, without folly—for you're not foolish,: be as active as you can and as you like . . . There's no reason why you shouldn't have a really splendid life.

The emotional disturbance is in Milly's unconscious and she cannot be jollied or reasoned out of her suffering. She goes to her physician the second time alone. Hadn't there been a lady with her on Wednesday? And isn't there Mrs. Stringham? Doesn't that make another friend?

MILLY: Yes, it makes another; but they all together wouldn't make—well, I don't know what to call it but the difference. I mean when one is—really alone. I've never seen anything like the kindness. Only one's situation is what it is. It's *me* it concerns. The rest is delightful and useless. Nobody can really help. That's why I'm by myself today. I *want* to be—in spite of Miss Croy, who came with me last. If you can help, so much the better—and also of course if one can, a little, one's self.

Milly has complete freedom.

MILLY: That's of course by itself a great boon; so please don't think I don't know it. I can do exactly what I like— anything in all the world. I haven't a creature to ask— there's not a finger to stop me. I can shake about till I'm black and blue. That perhaps isn't *all* joy; but lots of people, I know, would like to try it.

Her distinguished friend wishes her to appeal to as many sources of interest as possible and he wishes her also not to make, as she was perhaps doing, too much of her isolation. He does not recommend a change of climate.

SIR LUKE: Absolutely not; I "send" you nowhere. England's all right—anywhere that's pleasant, convenient, decent, will be all right. You say you can do exactly as you like. Oblige me therefore by being so good as to do it.

She can't flee from herself and travel is not a remedy, but neither is it prohibited. Sir Luke's prescription in a word is to *live*.

MILLY: When you talk of "life" I suppose you mean, mainly, gentlemen.

SIR LUKE (*after a moment during which she imagines him to be appreciating her raciness*): When I talk of life I think I mean more than anything else the beautiful show of it, in its freshness, made by young persons of your age.

With time and proper treatment a melancholic gloom may lift and the person recover his former balance; but while the morbid depression lasts there is often a danger of suicide. Early in the novel Milly and Mrs. Stringham are in Switzerland on an alpine height and Mrs. Stringham brings away from that occasion

> a conviction that the future was not to exist for her princess in the form of any sharp or simple release from the human predicament. It wouldn't be for her a question of a flying leap and thereby of a quick escape . . . She wouldn't have committed suicide; she knew herself unmistakably reserved for some more complicated passage.

The young New Yorker, slim, pale, angular, haggard, "of not more than two-and-twenty in spite of her marks, whose hair was somehow exceptionally red even for the real thing, which it innocently confessed to being, and whose clothes were remarkably black even for robes of mourning, which was the meaning they expressed," meets Merton Densher. He is handsome and charming, and she is obviously smitten.

Here then is someone capable of replacing in her affections the lost loved ones. But, as a complication, Merton is in love with Miss Croy. The latter, a witness of her new friend's state, perhaps has imagination enough to know what the attentions of her betrothed will mean to the American girl; and if she be a true friend she might prize the opportunity to help Milly get through this decisive emotional crisis in her life. In order to be kind to her, to lend Densher to her for a temporary liaison, she risks something precious to herself. But she is sure of her lover. So she lets her stricken friend believe that she doesn't immensely care for the young man. And Aunt Maud, who is unaware of Milly's illness but who observes her infatuation with this journalist she herself has no room for in her plans regarding Kate, much in a manner as she likes him, does what she conceives to be a good turn to everyone by throwing the fellow whenever she can in the way of the wealthy young American.

Doesn't Milly have any surmise about what sort of "trap" Kate has prepared for her? These are some words she delivers to her confidant; the reader may judge to whom she is really referring:

Isn't he beautiful and good too himself—altogether, whatever he may say, a lovely acquaintance to have made? You're just the right people for me—I see it now; and do you know what, between you, you must do? You must simply see me through. Any way you choose. Make it out together. I, on my side, will be beautiful too, and we'll be—the three of us, with whatever others, oh as many as the case requires, any one you like—a sight for the gods! I'll be as easy for you as carrying a feather.

Mrs. Stringham makes common cause to a certain extent with Mrs. Lowder but her allegiance is solely to her Milly, not at all to Kate.

Kate wasn't in danger, Kate wasn't pathetic; Kate Croy, whatever happened, would take care of Kate Croy.

MRS: STRINGHAM: When I say she knows I should say she's a person who guesses. But *she* doesn't matter, Milly.

MILLY: Nobody matters, Susie—nobody.

One commentator noted that "we do not bestow the term *dramatic* upon scenes and situations which fail to show a marked opposition of wills" and that this novel has the material of drama when considered as "the struggle of Kate Croy and Milly Theale for the heart of Merton—for that is what it comes to in spite of the beautiful unselfishness of Milly."

Kate it is who first calls Milly a dove for her innocence of the gradations of London society. The rich young American, as an outsider, "not hideously relative to tiers and tiers of others," has access to the most elevated circles and it's only decent to tell her.

KATE: My honest advice to you would be to drop us while you can . . . You mustn't pay too dreadfully for poor Mrs. Stringham's having let you in. She has the best conscience in the world; she's enchanted with what she has done; but you shouldn't take your people from *her*. It has been quite awful to see you do it.

Another likeness, that of a princess, is conferred by her attendant friend. "Mrs. Stringham was a woman of the world, but Milly Theale was a princess." It became definite for Milly, "even if not quite solid, that to treat her as a princess was a positive need of her companion's mind." And this metaphor is improved when the young girl from the great republic removes "her black dress, her white face, and her vivid hair" to Italy and installs herself under the high pictured ceiling of the Palazzo Leporelli.

MRS. STRINGHAM: She's lodged for the first time as she ought, from her type, to be; and doing it—I mean bringing out all the glory of the place—makes her really happy. It's a Veronese picture, as near as can be—with me as the inevitable dwarf, the small blackamoor, put into a corner of the foreground for effect. If I only had a hawk or a hound or something of that sort I should do the scene more honor. The old housekeeper, the woman in charge here, has a big red cockatoo that I might borrow and perch on my thumb for the evening.

Doubtless there are things that Mrs. Stringham doesn't have enough of. A beautifully romantic vision, however, hardly seems to be one of them.

Kate's plan is for Densher to give Milly the lift that may save her life; or at least to let her have before she dies some taste of happiness, a chance to love and be loved. She perhaps thinks that under these circumstances Milly may become capable of an act of generosity by which her own prospect of marriage will profit. Or at any rate this gains her time with Aunt Maud. Kate, upon being taken up by her aunt, and providing she makes no unacceptable marriage during this woman's lifetime, has doubtless the expectancy of inherited money. She may indeed have aspirations of coming into eventual possession of big ugly Landcaster Gate itself, with all its wasted finish and its massive and florid and overstuffed furnishings. She may also have not lost hope that in time her Aunt Maud can be brought round to consent to her marriage with Densher.

But Merton is weary of waiting, and it is his own immediate prospects that are of prime importance to him.

MERTON: Good God, if you'd only *take* me!

KATE: We've gone too far. Do you want to kill her?

MERTON: Kill, you mean, Aunt Maud?

KATE: You know whom I mean. We've told too many lies.

MERTON: I, my dear, have told none!

KATE: Thank you very much.

MERTON: Rather than lay myself open to the least appearance of it I'll go this very night.

KATE: Then go.

MERTON: I'll tell any lie you want, any your idea requires, if you'll only come to me.

Indubitably, after Kate and Mrs. Lowder leave Venice, Densher's position, alone with Milly, is delicate. It is present to him that the girl has loosened the fixation of her affections from their former dwelling place and has attached them upon himself with an intensity. And it is clear to the reader that any premature undermining of this object relationship while it is in a pathological state, and taking into account the girl's fierce pride, can only aggravate calamitously her internal conflict and weaken her will to live.

It wasn't a case for pedantry (*Densher muses*); when people were at *her* pass everything was allowed. And her pass was now, as by the sharp click of a spring, just completely his own—to the extent, as he felt, of her deep dependence on him. Anything he should do, or he shouldn't, would have reference, directly, to her life, which was thus absolutely in his hands—and ought never to have reference to anything else. It was on the cards for him that he might kill her—that was the way he read the cards.

Every day for a period of several weeks Densher makes a visit to Palazzo Leporelli, which Milly never leaves. As first excuse for his remaining in Venice he pretends a book he is doing.

He was vivid, for a moment, on the difficulty of writing quietly in London.

She is immediately full of interest, but when she plies him with questions concerning it he retracts.

I don't know, upon my honor, what I'm doing.

She twice proposes a return call upon him at his rooms, which he parries. After twenty days of his going to the palace at tea time have passed he is met by the information that the signorina is not "receiving." He learns from Mrs. Stringham that this is in consequence of news brought by Lord Mark.

Lord Mark, when he delivers his blow to Milly, when he tells her in effect that this commoner for whom, in her fool's

paradise, she refused him has been all the while engaged to
Miss Croy, intends the girl some humiliation, to be sure, in
return for his own, but no harm. He only means harm to
Densher, and good of course to himself; he thinks that may
follow.

MRS. STRINGHAM (*to Densher*): The good, he thinks, if he
has patience—not too much—may be to come. He doesn't
know what he has done to her. Only *we*, you see, do that.

But Milly, since the dreadful visit, "has turned her face
to the wall." A fundamental fact, inwardly known by each
but pushed deep down and kept there by a diplomacy, is
shaken to the social surface where it can no longer be ignored.
The great medical man has been sent for, of course. Densher
meets him at the station but doesn't accompany him to the
palace.

MERTON: I don't go there now.
SIR LUKE: Oh!

Within three days, responding to a tinkle of his bell, the
eminent man stands again before Merton in his doorway. It
passes through the young fellow's mind that "he had come,
as from Mrs. Stringham, to say how she might be saved," but
it is ascertained that he has looked his young man up merely
for a prowl or two and a turn about the city.

They walked together and they talked, looked up pictures
again and recovered impressions—Sir Luke knew just what
he wanted.

Densher never inquires of him the state of Milly's health.
On the station platform, before he departs to his London
obligations, the doctor has a parting word:

I shall come back within the month. I bring you a message
from Miss Theale. I'm commissioned to ask you from her
to go and see her.

Book Nine closes with Merton's assurance: "I'll go today."
Book Ten opens with a scene between Kate and her betrothed
three weeks later at Landcaster Gate, a stroke for which
James has been much criticized. "In his eagerness to have the
characters reveal themselves and to have the consequences of
action explain action, he has left out what should have been
the great scene of the book—Densher's last interview with
Milly (wrote one commentator) . . . this is one of the few
occasions on which he merits the accusation of bloodlessness."
Kate's plan presupposes on the part of her betrothed a quantity of good nature, but the young journalist, strongly
tempted, thinks he sees in the Italian city his way to peace
and plenty, and by a route other than Mrs. Lowder's comparatively inferior wealth. To this end misinterpretative
processes are at work within him: he begins to falsify unconsciously for the sake of his own show. The answers he receives
to his questions are read in the light of wilfully distorting
assumptions; and he makes an advantage of the things that,
"in the general misery of explaining," have been taken for
granted, as intelligent people, between them. There is an
extent to which *i*'s are not dotted between them, have been
left consciously undotted. The name of Milly's illness has
never in so many words been formally communicated to him.
His scheme accordingly is to convince himself that he doesn't
know what it is actually. In the light of a bodily ailment
Kate's plan is seen as frankly sinister, and therefore it becomes
a virtue not to put it through.

MERTON: He told her, the scoundrel, that you and I are
secretly engaged . . . She learned it, you see, too soon . . . And
she *had* felt sure—through everything we had done—of there
not being, between us, so far at least as you were concerned,
anything she need regard as a warning.

KATE: Wouldn't it have been possible then to deny the
truth of the information? I mean of Lord Mark's?

MERTON: And to lie myself, you mean, to do it? We *are*,
my dear child, I suppose, still engaged.

KATE: Of course we're still engaged. But to save her life—!

MERTON: I wouldn't have made my denial, in such conditions, only to take it back afterwards.

KATE: Oh, you would have broken with me to make your denial a truth? You would have "chucked" me to save your conscience?

MERTON: I couldn't have done anything else. So you see how right I was not to commit myself, and how little I could dream of it. If it ever again appears to you that I *might* have done so, remember what I say.

KATE: You have fallen in love with her.

MERTON: Well then, say so—with a dying woman. Why need you mind, and what does it matter?

KATE: For what then did Milly send for you?

MERTON: She believed, I suppose, that I *might* deny; and what, to my own mind, was before me in going to her was the certainty that she would put me to my test. She wanted from my own lips—so I saw it—the truth. But I was with her for twenty minutes, and she never asked me for it.

KATE: She never wanted the truth. She wanted *you*. She would have taken from you what you could give her, and been glad of it even if she had known it false. You might have lied to her from pity, and she have seen you and felt you lie, and yet—since it was all for tenderness—she would have thanked you and blessed you and clung to you but the more. For that was your strength, my dear man—that she loves you with passion.

MERTON: If it was, somehow, for *her* I was still staying, she wished that to end, she wished me to know how little there was need of it. And, as a manner of farewell, she wished herself to tell me so.

So as a moral solution of the problem, and to oblige her, he took the train for London. He leans heavily upon his literal veracity to save his honor, as he calls it, but at the expense of another sort of falsity: "the lie of the uncandid profession of a motive."

The report of Milly's death comes in a wire from Mrs. Stringham to Landcaster Gate on Christmas Eve. At the same time, the season of gifts, a letter in Milly's hand arrives from Venice for Merton. He suspects its contents without reading and carries it, seal unbroken, to Kate.

KATE: You'll have it all from New York.

A Densher with money is now face to face with Kate, and there is no hindrance to their marriage except for one fact: he has fallen in love with the dead girl. He gives the living to understand that it is she who must alone choose whether he shall accept the bequest.

KATE: You're afraid of *all* the truth. If you're in love with her without it, what indeed can you be more. And you're afraid—it's wonderful! —to be in love with her.

MERTON: I never was in love with her.

KATE: I believe that now—for the time she lived. I believe it at least for the time you were there. But your change came—as it might well—the day you last saw her: she died for you then that you might understand her. From that hour you *did*. And I do now. She did it *for* us. I used to call her, in my stupidity—for want of anything better—a dove. Well she stretched out her wings, and it was to *that* they reached. They cover us. . . There's but one thing that can save you from my choice: your word of honor that you're not in love with her memory.

MERTONS I'll marry you, mind you, in an hour.

KATE: As we were?

MERTON: As we were.

KATE: We shall never be again as we were!

"Notwithstanding a surpreme effort of James's art to endow Kate Croy with a mode of sensibility able to stand alone, self-justified," one commentator wrote, "we are not sure that she is anything better than a common little swindler." Kate, early in the novel, remarks that "it wouldn't be the first time she had seen herself obliged to accept with smothered irony other people's interpretation of her conduct. She often ended by giving up to them—it seemed really the way to live—the version that met their convenience."

THE AMBASSADORS

*In Boston, grand opera is now en-
dorsed by all the churches, and at-
tendance at the opera places no one's
morals under suspicion.*

BOSTON TRANSCRIPT (1909)

THE SUBJECT of *The Ambassadors* is the state of being of the
American who has bitten deep into the apple, as we may
figure it, of "Europe." The intensity of the case depends of
course upon the inward energy of the bite and the kind of
susceptibility involved in the act of tasting. The action is
mental primarily, it being for the "internal" that James
persistently tried. There is the case of the character prepared,
wherever presenting himself, only to judge and to feel
meanly, but a sense of the really fine subject disqualifies such
an emotional response as unsuited to be the proper center
of our interest. And all of the people in this novel do somehow, in one way or another, judge and feel meanly comparative to Strether, and they are in consequence all circum-
ferential figures assigned to the penumbra surrounding the
central light. The having of but one principal in the
composition who supremely matters and who alone holds
the main interest from beginning to end lends to this work
an *anecdotic* cast.

The anecdote consists, ever, of something that has oddly
happened to some one, and the first of its duties is to
point directly to the person whom it so distinguishes. He
may be you or I or any one else, but a condition of our
interest—perhaps the principal one—is that the anecdote
shall know him, and shall accordingly speak of him, as its
subject . . . The anecdote has always a question to answer—

57

of whom necessarily is it told? . . . To whom in the instance before us does the principal thing, the thing worth the telling, happen?

(JAMES, *Prefaces*)

The "hero" of the thing, the character primarily conceived and presented, is Strether. It is Strether's emotion for which this situation is valuable and which has chief call upon our attention throughout; the impingement of the experience upon his mind *makes* the subject. Of course one also, concomitantly, sees the author place the situation in the blest drama light, dramatically handle it as a straight action, but the manner in which the whole thing remains subject to the register, ever so closely kept, of the consciousness of but one of the actors in the offered play qualifies this novel as anecdotic in a degree exceeding either *The Wings of the Dove* or *The Golden Bowl.*

Round Lambert Strether *The Ambassadors* is systematically constructed, a character eminently fitted to take and keep the center of the stage, a man of sensitive perceptions, intelligent, humane, typifying the best elements of the New England race. New England, its old life and its old attitude, had produced and nourished him, and it is quite, for the story, as if he had thus been engendered and constituted to the particular end of extravagantly reacting from them. This change of mind becomes the novel's central development; in that subtle revolution the subject finds its dramatic climax: it is the history of a sentiment and its accepted catastrophe, or at least conversion.

Life for Strether has been an affair of living always in harness and in provincial conditions, and nevertheless, when no longer in his prime and still overworked, without having a great deal to show for it in the way of achievement, of acknowledged success, or money. He strikes himself as having come in for many of the drawbacks and perhaps discredit of unsuccess without, unfortunately, even much of the usually accompanying entertainment or personal adventure to look back on. He feels disenchanted without having known any great enchantments, enchanters, or, above all, enchantresses. He has missed out on "fun," been ridden by his "New England conscience" in a society so simply constituted that pleasure is deprecated, facilities for enjoyment scant and crude, and the business light supreme, business being places in which people sit close and make money. His past, insofar as it has not been grind, has seemed largely misadventure: the loss of his wife early, and then failure of sympathy with his little dull boy who also died young and whose temperament he has subsequently accused himself, with bitter compunction, of not having understood and allowed for, of having handled with insufficient tenderness and tact.

He has tried half a dozen things, experiments in various directions, without carrying them far, making little of them, and successively giving them up. There has been prolonged effort and tension in plenty, but not happily concentrated. Currently he is the conductor of a "high class" periodical, an expensive one that doesn't pay, is too enlightened to succeed commercially though not to "do good." Its subsidy is wholly provided by the widow of the local rich manufacturer, a man known to Strether in his time, and not agreeably, as the reverse of overscrupulous.

The widow herself, however, is very different and it is she who is now dominant in ownership and control of the considerable family business, the manufacture of some unspecified small article of familiar domestic use. Mrs. Newsome is devoutly conscientious, strenuously high-minded, nervous, "intense," full of social ideals and activities of a compensatory nature in respect to her late husband's hard, sharp career. Strether has helped her with her charities and reforms. He has been advisory about the thing to do and the thing not to, the way and the way not: he has been exactly the clever, competent man needed by a peculiarly high-strung woman, an influence making for the sanity and success of her good works. With his interest too in her subjects and ideals he has played straight into the current of Mrs. Newsome's earnest activities, the manifestations of the restless conscience that is in her in a measure unwittingly expiatory.

The *Review* is one of these benificent endeavors, not

frivolously literary but a group of articles devoted to serious questions and inquiries, economic, social, sanitary, humanitary. The woman gave Strether his chance at a given moment and he accepted it from her. His name as editor is on the green cover, where both of them have liked to see it. To be plain, she's in love with him. To say that he is in love with her would be to say too much, but he likes, admires, and esteems her. She is the "prominent woman" of Woollett, Massachusetts, a figure of much importance there with her name much in the local papers, and she is besides, other things: invalidical, though a particularly intense and energetic invalid, exalted and imperious, depressed and anxious, at once shrill and muffled, at once extremely abounding and extremely narrow, and of an austerity, a refined hardness and dryness of grain. Not an enchantress, decidedly, but the most remarkable woman, the most distinguished, within Strether's contracted social range.

Mrs. Newsome is slightly younger than Strether, who is fifty-five, and she has two children: a daughter of thirty, Mrs. Pocock, who lives in the same town as her mother and near her, in close communion with her, being married to a partner in the business; and a son, Chadwick, twenty-eight, who is a great source of anxiety. The young man upon inheriting considerable money from his maternal grandfather has gone more or less rapidly to the "bad" with it; that is to say he has gone to Paris. He became a slave of his passions from the moment he obtained the wherewithal to indulge them. He has been got hold of there by a dreadful Frenchwoman older than himself who is feeding on him and satisfying her lust with him and as to whom Mrs. Newsome is divided between the dread that he will marry her, which will be terrible, and the dread that he will go on living with her without marrying her, which will be more horrible still. She has her theory of his shocking conduct: it's all a dark spell cast upon him by the monstrous mercenary woman. To have withdrawn from his own country, not to have immediately launched himself in business of a rigorous sort, was to *be* exposed to the clutches of just such creatures.

Strether has also not been without his lights about Chad,

whom he has known a bit as a boy and in earlier youth. He has *his* theory about him, which differs from the mother's. The Chad he remembers was, alas, not a little of an egotist and even a brute. His own boy, at all events, hadn't been a brute. He had in all likelihood not even been dull, really; had been dull only in proportion as he had been neglected by the father who had, in those years, so insanely given himself to merely missing the mother. He aches with the sense that he himself was the brute—harshly, stupidly blundering in *that* doomed relation.

There is a business chance of importance awaiting Chad, one that cannot be much longer kept open for him, the organization and supervision of a new sales department for the concern. Between Paris and Woollett he has now absolutely to choose. The case is simple: perdition on one side; salvation on the other—spiritual and also, incidentally, financial. The young man, though, has quite failed to rise to the maternal reasoning, and has further certified his indifference to propriety by ceasing to answer her letters. Mrs. Newsome had a plan of going out after him but indispositions, nervousness, apprehensions, have checked this. So Strether, as the service of a loyal and grateful friend, has offered to go in her stead to see what, in the premises, he can do. They have both felt that it will have been, on the possible bad issue, but small honor to them if the boy be lost without some practical and personal effort to save him. The journey also fits in with a crisis in Strether's personal history that they think it may contribute to ease off or produce the evaporation of. He has been chronically deficient in holidays and is so distinctly fagged-out and in need of "a little change."

When Mrs. Newsome's agent arrives in the vast bright Babylon, Chad is out of town, so that Strether is for a time occupied just with the sense and image of the great city. Being away from home and without something immediately to do, some responsibility to meet, he has a large increase of the sense of rest and refreshment, change, long-deferred amusement and ease; he has a sense of emotional release, of escape from Woollett, its pressure of work suddenly lifted from his shoulders. The place of abode of Chad, on the

Boulevard Malescherbes, is tasteful and pleasant. Chad has
lent it for the term of his absence to a friend, a young American art student, John Little Bilham by name, who much
interests Strether as a product of the Paris art world, the
product of an air of which he has never yet, directly, tasted
a mouthful. He has a sort of lull with Bilham and others at
sidewalk cafés, at restaurants, theaters—the *Theatre Français,*
perhaps even the *Folies-Bergére.* There are facilities for
enjoyment in Paris, a high amenity, a general aesthetic and
social appeal. In Woollett the symbol of pleasure is the beer
saloon, or perhaps the amateur theatrical.

> Woollett isn't sure it ought to enjoy. If it were it would.
> But it hasn't, poor thing, any one to show it how.

The deficiency of Woollett is made vivid by the contrast
with Paris; its aesthetic bareness by the wondrous Louvre,
the old bookstalls by the Seine, the magnificent rightness and
beauty of the architecture, the chic dress of the people on
the boulevards in the bright early-spring weather. Paris has
art, and this is what now gives life for Strether an indispensable relish. He finds himself on quite other ground, in
richer air. The challenge here is in the fullness, not in the
meagerness, of aspects, and he gapes responsive to every
item: it is all a fresh revelation, an aesthetic adventure and
a deep joy, the flower of civilization at its finest. The great
dim social complexity is all bathed in the golden glow of the
city's scenic appeal, which makes almost a new light to see
by, the physical felicity of the face of Paris. Clearly, Paris
receives the palm for good looks. In Woollett there is the
gray street scenery of a factory town, a visual ugliness. Some
appreciative faculty in the old gentleman that has lain dor-
mant is awakened by Paris' beauty; it appeals by its most
inward principle to his taste; a hunger in him is gratified by
it; the suppressed artist in him is released by Paris; a new
dimension, in which he takes a critical delight, is introduced
to his life. He gathers in the fruits of his quickened sensibility; merely for his own wanton joy he indulges in a larger
draft of the wine of aesthetic perception than any he had ever
before owed to a single throb of that faculty.

Chad then, after a little, comes on the scene, but with more differences about him than Strether has expected, and not in the direction Strether has girded himself for. He has felt that there will probably be differences, marked ones, from the image remembered of the boy in his earlier time, as is indeed only natural, but he has feared that these will have consisted in a merely further coarsening of his primal crudity: he has expected to discover him brutalized, perverted, poisoned —all in some rather obvious and distressing way. Now, in his presence, he is relieved to find that the bracing he has put up has been needless. His manners at least have extraordinarily improved; there is no grossness of bad manners at all; and Chad is "easy" for him and in agreement with him to a degree that is a surprise. He has even improved in appearance; is handsomer than he had ever promised to be; not looking, as he had of old, only bold and wild. Surprising streaks of white already lend his hair a distinction, in contrast to Strether's own crop which in the evening of life is still black. Chad's look and manner is that of a man of the world, that of a man to whom things have happened and were variously known. He had been rough and now he is smooth. The note of the changed creature *is* strong in Chad—it overlies everything else for Strether: the young man presents himself as a prodigy in transformation, but in a progression the reverse of distressing.

Without delay Strether puts before Chad the business, Mrs. Newsome's, he has come out on. There's money, in quantities, in the family concern: it's a big brave bouncing business with quite a number of buildings, almost a little industrial colony. The late Newsome was a man of ideas in that particular line and gave the thing in his time such an impetus that his family derive a large income from it and will continue to do so if it can be made to continue to boom; if their interests are sharply guarded and its working thoroughly kept up. Chad has been glad enough of the money from Woollett's industry. He has had the free use of a great deal of this substance, a generous allowance having hitherto been granted him by his mother, and she has of course the resource of cutting her supply off. This money together with the quantity left him by his grandfather, which is also on no small scale, has been the basis for his life in Europe.

On Chad's head, at Woollett, certain high hopes are placed. He's of importance to the concern, or can easily become so if he will. There are signs of his having inherited a natural turn for business, and it will be much better if Mrs. Newsome has her own man in the firm. The thing has so developed that an opening that scarcely existed three years ago now simply waits for him, a place in the top management of the marketing "end." His mother has kept this for him, holding out against strong pressure. It requires, naturally, his being on the spot and making a big effort for a big result. To see that he doesn't miss it is what Strether has come out for. If he'll pull himself together, break with Paris and come home, he'll take up his material reward. He's at the parting of the ways. He can come into the business now—he can't come later. It's a question of an immediate rupture and an immediate return.

The youth displays some appetite for the facts and figures that Strether pours into him.

He made no crude profession of eagerness to yield, but he asked the most intelligent questions, probed, at moments, abruptly, even deeper than his friend's layer of information, justified by these touches the native estimate of his latent stuff, and had the air of trying to live, reflectively, into the square, bright picture.

He freely concedes that he *has* let himself go. But he's coming round—he's not so bad now. And he isn't entangled.

STRETHER: But our suppositions don't matter if you're actually not entangled.

CHAD: I never *was* that—let me insist. I always had my own way. And I have it at present.

STRETHER: Then what are you here for? What has kept you if you *have* been able to leave?

CHAD: Do you think one's kept only by women? Is that what they think at Woollett? I must say then you show a low mind!

He's here simply because he has *liked* to be. When he wants to go, no one will have any power to keep him.

CHAD: One doesn't know quite what you mean by being in women's "hands." It's all so vague. One is when one isn't. One isn't when one is. And then one can't quite give people away. I've *never* got stuck—so very hard; and, as against anything at any time really better, I don't think I've ever been afraid. Don't you know how I like Paris itself?

They haven't, at Woollett, got anything like Paris. He has two particular friends, however, two ladies, mother and daughter, that he wants Strether to meet, to know, and to like. He will oblige him by not bringing their business to a crisis till he has done so. They will be in town presently, coming back from an absence.

They're the best friends he has in the world, and they take more interest than any one else in what concerns him.

The young fellow, meanwhile, amiably and thoughtfully introduces Strether to other friends: he knows painters, sculptors, studios; knows a celebrity or two; puts his New Englander in relation with them—superficial, momentary, but very interesting to Strether—who enjoys it all to a degree almost scandalous. He brings about in particular an occasion of contact with a prime celebrity of a very special note, a first-rate artist or at least one who passes for such, the great Gloriani, who has all the appearance, the external marks and signs, and the fame. One charming Sunday in June Strether finds himself, with various other people, for an afternoon consecrated to "artistic and literary" talk in the celebrated sculptor's beautiful secluded garden in the heart of the Faubourg Saint Germain. It is all as new to Strether as it is picturesque and agreeable; a beautifully genialized, humanized, civilized, even romanticized thing. He yields to the seduction of so appointed a nook. But he can only feel, given the attractive strangeness of the place and people, the temper and tone of this life, its manners, speech, intercourse, in such a difference of milieu, extremely "out of it." And the "too late" comes immensely home to him: he makes out precious ingredients and influences at his age, as one who has had his time in the world, closed to him, forfeited and gone.

The occasion is a date for him, a picture and a message. Bilham is there, the young art student whom he likes, who is acuter, more "intellectual" and aesthetic than Chad, and he indulges himself so far as to warn Bilham not to commit *his* error, not to let the good days pass. He hasn't till now even suspected very much what he was losing; the alternative wasn't present to him. Europe has opened his eyes to unexpected importances and values; makes him feel his mistake. It's quite another and more congenial order of things, an atmosphere much more breathable. In Woollett culture is a thin trickle, but in Paris a flow. As he bathes initially, in its pleasant plash he thinks of Woollett as shrinkage, Paris as extension of life—so much more propitious to civilized development. Look at what it has made of such unpromising material as Chad! The miracle of the young man's redemption becomes for Strether the positive and living proof of what the civilizing process can do at its best even with comparatively poor clay.

It's in the beautiful Paris garden with its historic Old World atmosphere and amid a society of these different proportions that our hero's first introduction to Chad's two friends takes place. Mme. de Vionnet and her daughter are, happily, at last there, and they make upon him the greatest impression. The woman is indeed charming, he fully recognizes. She is young—that is, she is thirty-eight, bright, graceful, gracious, sympathetic, interesting; she *lends* herself to everything with the friendliest ease. She is not freshly young nor has she positive beauty but she has a face and a general air and aspect that singularly speak to him.

At bottom of it all, for him, was the sense of her rare unlikeness to the women he had known.

The woman is supremely an enchantress and fairly romantic for him. She is the person of most personal charm, indisputably, that the poor old gentleman has ever met, and he feels her nameless force at play. Her daughter, a girl of seventeen, is almost as much of a revelation in her own way and degree: a little tender flower of shy good breeding; different again from pretty little girls of seventeen as hitherto known to him.

Strether is seeing the new Chad in his European setting for the first time, seeing him in the golden light of Paris, and the world of Chad, as it is now immediately about Strether, has so bright an air of humanity and gaiety, of charity and humor, that the more he sees of it the less he finds it at all possible consistently to deplore and denounce. It's a society of refinement, graced by fine art, and governed by decorous but witty manners. Inward stirrings in Strether cause him to recognize this as a style of life that has a certain plausible side. The preference for ease, the play of the passions, the appetite for pleasure—they have not enough allowed for these influences and appeals at Woollett. Chad is free to do precisely as he likes with his life. Let him order it in his own way. His movements and his inclinations are his own affair. Chad's adoption of the aesthetic answer to the problem of existence needs no further defense than the fact that he is, by the turn of his mind, aesthetic. Not to be able to unfold from within is ill fortune. A man is always justified, save for cruelty, when he has succeeded in living the real life of his mind. To live this way, amid culture, art, intelligence, to enjoy and feel and learn amid a society that is the right society for one's self, is in itself a high form of success. To *be* this way, to appreciate and enjoy where there exist so much to be appreciated and enjoyed, is better than to *do* on the unglamorous plane, the grubbier side of life, at Woollett.

What is not charmlessly commercial in Woollett is too shrilly moral: all sacrifice and service to others, selflessness stressed to excess by Puritanism. Mrs. Newsome's achievements and her earnestness have been almost wholly in the moral order. Here is a society that is decent implicitly, not fanatically, and that doesn't scant and neglect the aesthetic and positively deprecate the sensuous. In Woollett morality is *flagrant,* a *conscious* propriety, a comparatively crude "uplift" that strikes him now as wanting in proportion and taste. Virtue is present in Paris but without emphasis, more sophisticated and casual, less stiff; character and conduct honorable enough but also enjoyable. Hortatory preaching is displaced by a suggested appeal to the finer part of the mind. Paris is positively gay; bristling and bustling and resonant; yet untouched by the strenuous note. How little this Parisian social air conduces to the formation of prigs. Woollett is joyless: all straight and narrow insistences, and with a poverty, a bare provinciality of life.

He had come out to save the barbarians and instead has been converted by them. It is he, in his innocence, that is the barbarian, he feels, and Paris the later state of culture, sophisticated but not decadent, life at a higher intensity, a luxury of life, of sensibility. He is absorbing all that Paris is giving him as nutriment. He feels himself to be quite the edified party, and his old importances are reduced to make room for new values, ones not counting for much at Woollett, other dignities and claims, other social and human positions. There are not enough of these things at Woollett and they are not fair enough to engage happily the finer attention. They grub with a good conscience at Woollett, but that leaves them short hours for leisure and for cultural acquisition of a free sort.

Such is the revolution that takes place in Strether, and Mme. de Vionnet has in it an enormous value, becomes its most determinant cause—becomes so simply by being, and by showing herself, exactly what she is. She emphasizes with the charm of her presence the essence of what the old gentleman has lacked where he came from and what he therefore finds so delightful, new and different in Paris. *She* is better than anything. He finds in her more merits, more womanly worth. She fixes for his senses their supreme symbol of the fair. She comes to stand for him for most of the things that make the *charm* of civilization at its sublimest, as he now revises and imaginatively reconstructs civilization. And since it's clearly she that is most responsible for Chad's improvement, for the enlargement and enrichment of his personality, Strether's theory of a rescue *from* such a person is discom-

posed, and with it the cogency of his position as Mrs. Newsome's ambassador to Paris.

Mme. de Vionnet and "Europe" so act, stage by stage, upon
the old gentleman's perceptions that Chad's relative importances, assumed and acted upon, as Strether now sees
them, appear the reverse of lamentable. The deprecatory
attitude quite drops and is replaced by the benedictory. The
young man's refined and intelligent preference for Paris over
Woollett, its polar opposite, its plain and dry antithesis,
according to Strether's new sense of the matter, is rather to
be congratulated and encouraged. The higher distinction
is in Paris and the larger chances and connections. The lad
already has these within his grasp. The youth's Parisian
opportunity represents to Strether an enviable state of affairs,
a happiness, an escape from boresome drudgery to all the
materially and mentally agreeable in life. It would be stupid
and ignoble of the fellow not, with his chance, to follow the
aesthetic and sensuous clue, which has so raised the whole
possibility of living, for Strether's eyes, into a higher sphere
of light and grace; and, with his already so luckily ample
fortune, to throw it up just to follow the money-monster.

He undergoes a reversal of role, a total transformation in
purpose, and makes Chad the opposite appeal, the appeal that
will cause him to pass for some unspeakable kind of traitor
at Woollett. Strether wouldn't, were *he* Chad, go back to
New England and spend the better part of his life doing
advertising—which has already, upon ceasing to be content-
edly but announcement and information, blossomed into a
new form of mediocrity. It's too late for the old gentleman
to "go in" for Paris, the sense of exclusion from all he would
have liked most to enjoy in life is strong in him, but at least
he can advise the young fellow in the right way as he now so
sharply sees it. This will be the great thing he can still do.

Chad has an independent command of means sufficient to
his needs: he's not money-dependent upon Mrs. Newsome.
The fortune inherited from his grandfather is enough to
live on in Paris in pleasant material conditions. Here he will
have time for the free development of his faculties in a sympathetic, stimulating environment. Life at Woollett is of the

dullest and bleakest: a social order in which every one is hurled straight upon an office or store with the injunction of rising. "Culture" in Woollett is of the thinnest, whereas all about Strether in Paris it is by every appearance almost glutinously thick. To live, on whatever terms, in this thickness, to feel and to think in it, seems precious. A life the most richly consequent should rise and grow straight out of these fertilizing conditions; but one of "no practical account" by Woollett's categories of appreciation and perception. New England finds its main ideal in a "strict attention to business," that is to buying and selling. To attend strictly to business is to be invariably *there*, on a certain spot in a certain place; just as to be nowhere in particular, to *have* to be nowhere, tells the queer tale of a lack or of a forfeiture, or possibly even of a state of intrinsic unworthiness. Disconnected from business in New England, one can only be connected with the negation of it, which has as yet no affirmative, no figurative side. At Woollett if Chad doesn't immerse himself in the family business, certainly he will have no accepted place. Material vindication, acquisition, reward in the form of dollars and cents, what is called success generally is overemphasized in America—the old supposition of profit, or in other words the old sense of pleasure. Here in Paris is pleasure itself, the finer profit, intenser experience, and precious mental acquisition. And since Chad already *has* money—he's even rich!—a life both ampler *and* easier is workable so easily. The charm of "Europe" added to his happy finances results in an almost complete absence of difficulty, a blest exemption from social pressures and economic stresses. What does he want more?

As Strether sees it, Chad has the means and faculties to try for a higher form of success than the commercial. Here in Paris, at the very seat and heart of culture, as this is so imperfectly understood and sought in Woollett, his aesthetic and intellectual interests will be fed by congenial surroundings and people, and this is to be preferred over being *in* New England without being *of* it. In America, with its differences of measure, its so narrow and rigid standards and convictions, such beatitude on the part of the blandly idle and the supposedly accomplished is deprecated—denounced as a departure from the career of business, of industry and respectability, the so-called regular life. But the "cult of industry" pales to poor tired Strether before the new sense of the life of leisured culture, the life spent in educating and enjoying oneself on a level undreamt of by Woollett. To settle to any career, to ply any trade, is "narrowing" for comprehensive culture, but to surrender to flat, tasteless advertising would be a weak and foolish, a really appalling waste of time.

There is a material advantage involved, one large enough not to be too lightly sacrificed, and making this special situation. Yet about such a renouncement there might hang, for Strether, a moral glamor. And with Chad already "comfortably fixed," loss of the pecuniary advantages accruing needn't be worth speaking of; not when other sympathies redress the balance. And Paris tips the scale for Strether. Above all, he sees Mme. de Vionnet as worth having and keeping for a friend. If the question of a so-called misspent or wasted life comes up, one with nothing greatly worth-while achieved in it, he can only look back on his own in Woollett, what he made of it and what he missed, working hard yet getting nowhere, and the possibilities of his own youth that had long ago been stunted on the scant soil and withered by the cold winds of Puritan New England.

STRETHER: Is it for her to have turned a man out so wonderfully, too, only for somebody else? When it's for each other that people give things up they don't miss them. Let them face the future together!

BILHAM: You mean that, after all, he shouldn't go back?

STRETHER: I mean that if he gives her up—!

BILHAM: Yes?

STRETHER: Well, he ought to be ashamed of himself.

It is surely mean, in the light or the dusk of all that Strether now sees, to conclude that the relation of Mme. de Vionnet and Chad is indecent. Strether is now ashamed of the grotesquerie of the description of Chad that he had at

a distance made out so luridly as the young man's necessary
state, and the presumable depravity he and Mrs. Newsome
together had hugged the conception of as the color of the
lad's connection with Mme. de Vionnet. He has smiles for
the naïveté of the bundle of coarse, lurid, vulgar notions
with which he started from home. It's a totally and splendidly
different affair from what they had feared in Woollett. The
woman, who is a countess, and her lovely daughter are simply
the best of the young man's friends and have made for him a
pleasant second home. It's a privilege to be as Chad is with
ces dames, who weren't at all likely to have taken up with
one of his type. The thing is an anomaly, no doubt, but that
doesn't diminish the value that Strether sets on it, the value
of such a relation, for any young man, as such a woman as
Mme. de Vionnet represents. The daughter is engaged to a
young Frenchman of "position" and Chad has had the chief
hand in making the marriage arrangement. The mother is
living apart from her husband, the obnoxious Comte de
Vionnet. The pair are on irreconcileable terms but they
belong to the kind of *monde* that, in France, doesn't divorce.

> She's a tremendously clever, brilliant, capable woman,
> and with an extraordinary charm on top of it all . . . It
> isn't every clever, brilliant, capable woman that has it. In
> fact it's rare with any woman. So there you are. I under-
> stand what a relation with such a woman—what such a
> high, fine friendship—may be. It can't be vulgar or coarse,
> anyway—and that's the point.

Mme. de Vionnet and Chad, face to face with Strether in
Paris, place themselves in the right perspective for his ap-
probation; and they do it, they satisfy him that the attachment
is virtuous and the allegation against them made at Woollett
is baseless, simply by showing themselves with all the right
grace and the right assurance. The felicity for Strether is that
while the difference from Woollett all round him is immense
the embarrassment of it is nil—as if the getting into relation
with "Europe" and with Mme. de Vionnet with the least
waste had been prepared from so far back that a sort of divine

economy now fairly ruled. When put in presence of the aesthetic, if one *is* aesthetic, one understands.

But Strether cannot establish to Mrs. Newsome's satisfaction that her moral indictment of Chad is without foundation. A transformed Chad is such a large imaginative jump, one of which the lady in Woollett is unabashedly incapable. She is of course galled and humiliated by his attitude and not a little puzzled by his betrayal and by its appearing now to be *he* that is in peril of perdition. The complication is one that takes, so far as she is concerned, a good deal of explaining, and, though he tries, there are things he *can't* explain. The precious pair are not spoiled for him by his analysis of their situation, but what is spoiled is his freedom of communication with Mrs. Newsome.

For Mrs. Newsome it is all hideously wrong and must remain so, and to her Strether appears to be obscurely afflicted. The woman whose attachment he supposes virtuous is obviously Chad's mistress. The situation described amounts to an implication of that supreme fact. The innocence is Strether's in seeing the matter thus, not Chad's and Mme. de Vionnet's—this view that he considers more enlightened and sophisticated. Her wayward son is caught in the toils of a vile enchantress—a charmer and playmate, of a thoroughly superior kind, no doubt—who is pulling his money out of him and detaining him in idleness in Europe to his hurt. Mme. de Vionnet *isn't* a Value, a hard, fine, firm *worldly* value at all by the real measure of such calculations and imaginations as Mrs. Newsome's. Her son, whose bad habits have always so worried her, requires, as usual, to be taken in hand, adjured to break off his base entanglement and give up his pointless life of lounging about Europe as a gentleman of leisure with a mistress. So grand a manner of existence as this now appears to Strether, the first lady of Woollett, with her views, was to find no grace in so long as she lived. The trampish glamor of it is forever beyond her moral taste or sympathy; an effete and depraved substitute for living that money from Woollett has made possible, income unearned by Chad. The object of her parental interest is to be brought back home where his time and talent may be employed in useful and remunerative work, the kind of work the fellow is cut out for by his parts. At this crisis of his career she expects her emissary, the friend whose soundness and discretion she had relied upon, not to abet and encourage her son in wrongdoing but to drive home the necessary point to the erring youth, explain to the reprobate the emptiness of his sort of life and the importance of his getting settled at productive work of some social service. Objurgations are in order. Chad is a case toward which sternness alone now wouldn't be sinister.

Mrs. Newsome sends her intimate friend and deputy a cable: if Chad won't come, he's to leave him; Strether's to come at any rate himself. If he doesn't immediately sail, the Pococks will immediately come out.

A FRIEND (*to Strether*): You've cabled?

STRETHER: No—I've made Chad do it.

FRIEND: That you decline to come?

STRETHER: That *he* declines. We had it out this morning, and I brought him round. He had come in, before I was down, to tell me he was ready—ready, I mean, to return. And he went off, after ten minutes with me, to say he wouldn't.

FRIEND: Then you've *stopped* him?

STRETHER: I've stopped him. That is for the time. That is where I am.

STRETHER: I simply said to him: "I want to stay, and the only way for me to do so is for *you* to." That I wanted to stay seemed to interest him, and he acted on that.

FRIEND: He wants then himself to stay.

STRETHER: He half wants it. That is he half wants to go. My original appeal has to that extent worked in him. Nevertheless he won't go. Not, at least, so long as I'm here.

FRIEND: But you can't stay here always. I wish you could.

STRETHER: By no means. Still, I want to see him a little further. He is not in the least the case I supposed; he's quite another case. And it's as such that he interests me. I don't want to give him up.

It is through Strether's delegated sensibility that we receive our report, as the mind from which the best interest in the material is to be squeezed, the one a good deal more interesting artistically than any of the others in the book. The dramatic presentation of his frame of mind is the controlling idea, the central interest of the work, the theme round which the whole is organized. The novel is all his story, the story of the change in his thinking, and his point of view is "turned on" like a lamp from beginning to end, rendered moment by moment as action, for its rich psychological interest. The vision of things maintained is that of a man with arrears of personal history to make up; his actions are those of a spirit for which life, or for which at any rate freedom, had been too much postponed, treating itself at last to a luxury of experience. The meaning of his attitude is to be comprehended as some deep-down reaction, some extremity of indifference and defiance, of a character too long pressed and prescribed to, to which "Europe" gives a lift, lends him wings which without its greatness might have failed him.

STRETHER: I never had the benefit at the proper time—which comes to saying that I never had the thing itself. I'm having the benefit at this moment; I had it the other day when I said to Chad, "Wait"; I shall have it still again when Sarah Pocock arrives. It's a benefit that would make a poor show for many people; and I don't know who else but you and I, frankly, could begin to see in it what I feel. I don't get drunk; I don't pursue the ladies; I don't spend money; I don't even write sonnets. But nevertheless I'm making up late for what I didn't have early. I cultivate my little benefit in my own little way. It amuses me more than anything that has happened to me in all my life. They may say what they like —it's my surrender, it's my tribute, to youth. One puts that in where one can—it has to come in somewhere, if only out of the lives, the conditions, the feelings of other persons. Chad gives me the sense of it, for all his gray hairs, which merely make it solid in him and safe and serene; and *she* does the same, for all her being older than he, for all her marriageable daughter, her separated husband, her agitated history. Though they're young enough, my pair, I don't say they're, in the freshest way, their *own* absolutely prime adolescence; for that has nothing to do with it. The point is that they're mine. Yes, they're my youth; since somehow, at the right time, nothing else ever was. What I meant just now therefore is that it would all go—go before doing its work—if they were to fail me.

To look at these things more closely, Chad has a social tone that he has picked up in Europe, in all probability under Mme. de Vionnet's tutelage: he has more formed and finished manners, a man-of-the-world ease and courtesy. This outward polish, in itself a matter of comparative minor importance, Strether thinks to be a sure sign of inner distinction. Rather, he has a choice of suppositions: either assume these surface manners to be civilized hypocrisies and bland deceits, or else take them for genuine; and he knows which view of the young man's deportment most agrees with his spiritual stomach. In the absence of proof to the contrary he can accept them as sincerities, and such a view would give it all a sense for which the roused appetite in Strether's spirit now aches and sighs. It is open to him to seize at anything that, from hour to hour, from day to day, keeps him going, leads him on and on in this new delightful direction. "Europe" appeals so to Strether's finer fibres of appreciation that any distressful assumptions, which can be no more than guesses or hunches, find themselves unwelcome. He serenely dispenses with more conclusive evidence. The manner of Chad's own allusions to the things about him will have to suffice; such signs and tokens as his well-bred ease and his right light tone about the circumjacent charm he has gone in for, and the supereminence of some of his friends. He takes Chad on trust; he has a positive desire to take him on trust after Paris and reaction have artfully begotten in him a disposition. There is no basis of opinion without a basis of vision. That is to say, on grounds that have little to do with the data, the old gentleman adopts the supposition that is consonant with his present inward tone. *There* is the interest: in the intensity and plausibility and variety of the irrelevance.

Chad travelled to Europe in his youth and drained there the cup of pleasure: subsided easily into an existence of idle play and fornication. Strether also, in a first lift of enthusiasm for Paris, with his extreme apprehending sensibility to it, has taken the twist, sipped the poison; though in his case the only form of riot or revel possible is that of the visiting mind. Strether more subtly embodies the same "fatal" effect of European temptations or opportunities on characters giving way too freely of which Chad is an example in more vulgar form. Yet it is not that, with his changed consciousness, the holiday having acted too well, the old gentleman views life in rapport with Chad, simply as enjoyment on a high level and Paris as the place that provides it—although to react *from* the idea of grubbing and grinding one's youth away is to react *into* the hedonistic philosophy at least in part. Paris *has* spoiled Woollett for him, or him for Woollett, but the basic makeups of the two, Strether's and Chad's, are fundamentally different, and it is Strether's that is the finer frame of mind.

Strether is himself blameless in moral character, in the personal conduct of his own affairs. Europe is a demoralizing influence on him but it is also a cultural illumination. His is the mind most sensitive to the values of both worlds and the one capable of rising to Europe's better part. The old gentleman is of an artistic bent. His variegated employments at Woollett have never included touching the business. Even in the place of its manufacture he had refused to burn incense to the small domestic article. When he comes to Europe he takes it hard. Paris is a "larger" world, a social system that allows more for the exceptional and the eccentric, and for experiment in living. All his roused response goes out to its aesthetic appeal and to a social life at what at least seems to him a higher cultural level, a social setting with which he has a stronger affinity. If he is thrown off balance and disproportionately prizes charm and sensuous appeal when he first tastes such delights that is because of his issue from the opposite conditions, the unalluring appearance and the meagre aesthetic resources and inclinations of Woollett, and its narrow ethic, a lack there of certain things that make the amenity of human life. He overvalues in Paris what are scarce commodities at Woollett: His temperament has been subjected to repression and privation prolonged over half a century. He becomes a case of the human spirit long suppressed and then "exploding" when released.

Reader attention is centered on Strether—the author sticks to this as the rule of rules—and on Chad and his affair with Mme. de Vionnet only as they touch upon the old gentleman. And the point of interest in Strether which has made him the subject of James's pen is this transformation of feeling produced by the cultural illumination of Europe and the charm of Mme. de Vionnet, and the elevated vision they inspire him to take of Chad's affair. He is exalted by Europe, and—partly by associational magic—he takes an exalted view of Chad. The old New Englander gives himself a vicarious satisfaction by imaginatively identifying himself with Chad, that is with Chad in amended form, Chad given the benefit of the most admirable reasons for his conduct, those for which Strether can legitimately feel enthusiasm. Strether has a new richer view of life's possibilities for himself, one that he sees as now too late for himself, unsuited to his time of life, but that he thinks Chad, the *new* Chad, is capable of realizing. He's acting with superlative intended benignity and understanding toward the lad. He wants to befriend him and to do him justice, which he hadn't done to his own son. It's as a delightful act of intelligence and justice that he extends to the youth his respect for what he is doing. And the young fellow's self-esteem, already a very considerable quantity, is bolstered by Strether's general sense that he has succeeded in growing too civilized for the perceptive old New Englander to find it in his responsible conscience to urge as a substitute for a continuation of that process a mere relapse to Woollett and business, in particular the shabby commercialism of advertising.

The question is what this young man of twenty-eight shall "do." As Strether sees it, Paris is the place for intellectual and aesthetic stimulation, and he regards the cultivation of this as profession and career enough. He exhorts Chad to make the great renunciation of business opportunity, of family, and of marriage so that he may continue in Europe for his further development and remain close to Mme. de Vionnet. He sees Chad as bettered by Europe, as distinctly good. He attributes a very high ideal of conduct to him—sufficient moral strength to withstand leisure and accept the responsibility of freedom, not to misuse it in large quantities. Strether himself has never known an excess of freedom. Those of the smaller sort never use all the freedom they have—which is the sign, exactly, by which we know them, but those of the greater have never had too much immediately to use —which is the sovereign mark of their felicity.

The transfiguring light in which Strether has now bathed Chad is largely of the old New Englander's own making and is imbued with his own tone and texture, ignoring radical dissimilarities of temperament and outlook between the two. Had the fellow but the intrinsic faculties Strether imputes to him, those which Bilham does possess, he might really celebrate the young man's stay in Europe as something proper and to be desired. Chad, however, is a man of a different make: what he is not is a person of genuine artistic or intellectual abilities, ambitions, or inclinations. Actually, Chad is neither addicted to the arts nor endowed for them. He isn't studying anything in Paris. The lad is not represented as having about him any paraphernalia of writing or painting or music or whatever. What the young man has been positively interested in, been all the while occupied with, is simply a disencumbered and irresponsible "good time." Except for his "head for business" there is nothing exceptional about him. The old New Englander's admiration is built upon a mistaken identity, upon erroneous conclusions as to what his distinction is and what his preferences are. The field of activity that is congenial to Chad's personality and talents and in which he has qualifications for functioning with professional competence, indeed in which he shows promise of becoming exceedingly proficient, is the business.

We see Chad in the "dialog," by what he *says,* and also in what he *does,* as Strether is confronted with it. By his actions and in scraps of remark his mind is revealed indirectly, registered dramatically, presented from the outside, as are the minds of all the others except Strether's. And James, with his usual virtuosity of innuendo, renders its inner vulgarity wonderfully, makes it dramatically clear. Chad's not crude and dull and boorish, but clever and plausible and agreeable and diplomatic; he's everything but sincere and straight; and everything toward Mme. de Vionnet but truly caring for her. As to theories and presumptions of what shall prove best for him, the remedy would be mostly psychological, a change of attitude, and although he is doubtless obtaining more sensuous education in Paris with Mme. de Vionnet, if he is susceptible of the enrichment of his spiritual soil he is in need of to live better, it is his mother, the lady who is essentially all moral pressure, who cares for spiritual decency unspeakably more than for anything else, who will enlighten him most about the fundamental decencies, who will try to rouse whatever sense of duty is latent in him, who will foster the *other* growth, the one not being fostered in him in Paris, that of moral beliefs and tastes, and who will be good for him. With the advantage of proximity to her his conduct will be criticized, taken a disparaging view of, and not applauded, the immaturity of his thinking and living will be sharply pointed out. It is she that, by conviction and example, suggests those traits in the moral quarter, as the basis of conduct, without which living is not of a quality worth while. For Mrs. Newsome virtue is a social grace and value, and this is a matter on which pretexts for ambiguity of view and of measure are as little as possible called upon by her cold reserves and her rigidly high standards to flourish.

The business is the paternal heritage to Chad. It is also what has enabled Newsome's widow to render her signal services to Strether, as well as to diffuse her conspicuous general benefits. But Strether has known the late Newsome and been well aware of what, in his character and practices, he didn't like about him, and his widow is a woman rich in just those connections that now have grown more ugly and smell more badly for him. However, Mrs. Newsome's money was not ill-gotten by *her*. In the midst of her husband's doings, and profiting by them, *she*, at least, had remained exquisite. And since she has been in control, the business is conducted honestly. They are making in Woollett a homely but useful article better than other people can, or at any rate *do*. She is also represented as a rich woman intensely conscious of her social responsibilities.

Mme. de Vionnet has done Chad a service; he is indebted to her for alterations, for the state of grace to which, by Strether's supposal, she has lifted him. (She has already changed Strether's own state too, his beguiled, his aesthetic.) It becomes thereby part of the young man's duty and honor, as well as his interest, not to desert her. To do so would be for him to violate the *moral* requirements of his situation.

STRETHER: The fact remains, nevertheless, that she has saved him.

BILHAM: I thought that was what *you* were to do.

STRETHER: I'm speaking—in connection with her—of his manners and morals, his character and life. I'm speaking of him as a person to deal with and talk with and live with—speaking of him as a social animal.

BILHAM: And isn't it as a social animal that you also want him?

STRETHER: Certainly; so that it's as if she had saved him *for* us.

BILHAM: It strikes you accordingly then as for you all to save *her?*

STRETHER: Oh, for us "all"!—They've accepted their situation—hard as it is. They're not free—at least she's not; but they take what's left to them. It's a friendship, of a beautiful sort; and that's what makes them so strong. They're straight, they feel; and they keep each other up. It's doubtless she, however, who, as you yourself have hinted, feels it most.

There is the discomfort of an attachment to a person one can never hope short of a catastrophe, or a boon of Providence, to marry. M. de Vionnet may live forever. Not being able to marry is all the pair have with any confidence to look forward to. A liaison with Mme. de Vionnet is adulterous at least technically and means estrangement from the fellow's mother and sister. Moreover, it's a denial to Chad of the normal relationships of marriage and children. The youth has his possible future before him. He has natural gifts for business, marked ones, and an opportunity to use these talents in the family concern awaits him, with large material advantages accruing. Nevertherless Strether counsels him to make this great renunciation. It's a case for a high line. It would be too odious, too base to abandon Mme. de Vionnet. And he would, besides, be giving up more than he would gain. It's more beautiful for the pair to keep on as they are.

Strether's assumptions about the morals of Chad, the qualities of character he introduces as now central in him, are no more to be derived from the way the young man is passing the time in Europe than they were from any purity of antecedent conduct; from what he has known of the fellow as a boy that does not inspire one with due confidence. Nor is what the New Englander has inferred about the lad's spiritual whereabouts and intentions verified by Chad's placid announcement of his readiness to go home and go into the business, and hence to leave Mme. de Vionnet. (This announcement was made subsequent to Strether's conversation with Bilham reported just above.) Strether's view of Chad is essentially the work of his imagination; its an agreeable fantasy, a pleasant fiction built up out of false premises, ones that dissimulate both the fellow's real abilities and his real character. As to *why* the old gentleman is imagining Chad as wholly other than what he is and so carrying on in the midst of the actual a process of mental obliquity, of self-delusion, there is an unavowed consideration affecting him, a camouflaged but powerful psychic force in the deeper currents of life, that tends to warp his judgment, makes him unwilling to look certain facts in the face. He refuses subconsciously to admit the true state of affairs.

Mme. de Vionnet excites an interest in Strether by her charm and intelligence, and she inspires a sympathy in him with her predicament. But she does much more. He is entranced by her: the spell she casts upon his spirit with her first assault is stronger than any it is possible for her to weave

over Chad's. Her effect upon the old New Englander is that
of an overwhelming love philter; and this unavowed passion
makes the basis, the mechanism, or the logic of his unsound
conduct in the affair. He has fallen in love with Mme. de
Vionnet, and this is the reason at the bottom, the one in the
passional secret places of life, for his credulous disposition
toward the young man's affair with her; and it is the prime
motive of why he has leaped to so baseless a view about Chad,
and still more why he clings to this view with a tenaciousness
and an unlimited good faith warranted neither by the youth's
past performance nor by the present data. It is Mme. de
Vionnet that is the truest center of Strether's new perceptions and his sweet aesthetic surrender. She is more the pivot
of the old New Englander's revolution than she is that of
Chad's.

A FRIEND: (to Strether): Are you really in love with her?
STRETHER: It's of no importance I should know. It matters
so little—has nothing to do, practically, with either of us.

He does not understand or admit to himself the real motive
for his judgments and actions; he is not aware of the importance of recognizing this for an upright attitude of mind.
He believes his advice and conduct in the affair simply to be
intelligent and disinterested behavior. He imagines himself
to be acting nobly, regardless of the consequences to himself
of his intervention in such a sense, at this moment of crisis
in the life of the young man. He doesn't himself disengage
the erotic motive. His rationalizations enable him to appear
in his own eyes, by doing so, to the highest advantage.

On the other hand, there is a total absence of danger that
Chad's loyalty will exceed the interest or worthiness of its
object. The moderate opinion of Mme. de Vionnet that the
younger man entertains he plainly enough indicates. The
primary fact to be grasped is that three main erotic ties
demonstrate themselves: one from Mrs. Newsome to Strether;
one from Strether to Mme. de Vionnet; and one from Mme.
de Vionnet to Chad—but that none of these emotional drives
show equal power in the reverse direction.

Strether's liability of succumbing to the kind of appeal that Mme. de Vionnet is capable of making has been greatly facilitated (to say it again) by his issue from such opposite conditions: an over strenuousness of work that leads to exhaustion and breakdown, too much repression and privation, too much discipline and restraint, moralism carried to extremes of narrowness, overdone idealism provoking in reaction, in respect to Woollett and industry, some total and excessive renouncement. He is experiencing the thrill of an act of insurrection against Mrs. Newsome and Woollett, a protest against the meagerness of the sensual aspect of their lives. He's an elderly man who hasn't "lived" or enjoyed in the sense of sensations, passions, impulses, pleasures; has lived only for duty and conscience, for pure appearances and daily tasks, for effort, surrender, abstention, sacrifice; and when transported to a different society he has given way to a wave of reaction against his old feelings and habits. This is a pitfall situation for a person of his sensibility and antecedent circumstances. Strether has now some blest independences of perception and judgment from Mrs. Newsome; a new freedom of range for an intellectual adventure; and he is delighted by this liberty of thinking and acting independently of the woman. Everything that takes place in Woollett takes place around Mrs. Newsome, and sort of in her interest. He is enjoying a certain defiance of her now from a superior height, as he believes, as well as from a safe distance. Mrs. Newsome interests Strether, but she doesn't fascinate.

There is nothing intimately personal for Mme. de Vionnet to expect from Strether, nor for him to expect from her. He has found this *femme du monde,* on short and superficial acquaintance, remarkably attractive, but she is nothing to himself, a mere lurking figure in Chad's background. His own close personal ties have all been with Mrs. Newsome. If he raises with Chad questions both of duty toward a woman and of self-interest, what of his own: what service, in such a life of helping others, is Strether rendering this lady that he has known and respected and liked from early days, and to whom he owes his present position at Woollett, who is prepared to guarantee and protect his future there, and to whom his relation has practically become an engagement?

STRETHER: (*to Mme. de Vionnet*): I've had but one thing to do—to put our case before him. To put it as it could only be put, here, on the spot—by personal pressure. My dear lady, my work, you see, is really done, and my reasons for staying on even another day are none of the best. Chad's in possession of our case and professes to do it full justice. What remains is with himself. I've had my rest, my amusement and refreshment; I've had, as we say at Woollett, a lovely time. Nothing in it has been more lovely than this happy meeting with you in these fantastic conditions to which you've so delightfully consented. I've a sense of success. It's what I wanted. My getting all this good is what Chad has waited for, and I gather that if I'm ready to go he's the same.

But Strether doesn't withdraw from the scene. He lingers on in Paris, and the reason he gives himself and others is that he wants to have the courage of his new convictions and see the situation through. He is not able to act in any other way.

MME. DE VIONNET: You can't in honor not see me through because you can't in honor not see *him*.
STRETHER: No, I can't in honor not see him.

There is something not altogether rational, an obsession or compulsive quality, in what Strether considers that Chad is morally obligated to do for Mme. de Vionnet, make a general sacrifice to her and a general repudiation of everything else, even while positing no sexual relation between them. And in the event of the latter there is the fundamental impropriety of their situation. Strether is not "obliged" to work so actively and intensely for Mme. de Vionnet to his own hurt, the wreck of his own fortunes with the lady at home to whom he has been attached, and it's in fact explainable only by an erotic fascination. The basis is psychological rather than logical. He's acting out of some deep inward necessity or perversity. Her spell has worked; she has charmed him thoroughly; and the effect has been produced. The emotional reference of all Strether's actions is to Mme. de Vionnet, and the removal of the young man is a service that Chad's mother's emissary grows increasingly less and less ready to perform. He tacitly shifts his loyalty to the Frenchwoman, suffers himself to become *her* confederate, and ceases to figure in that character to Mrs. Newsome, winds up as an active force *against* this lady in Woollett. In working for Mme. de Vionnet he obtains an emotional fulfillment. He is saving the beloved; and the hero, by definition, is one who saves, and who does so at loss or risk to himself.

Chad however, is not keen for sacrifices and great renunciations. He has abandoned himself to a life directed only by his sensual pleasure, a useless life of self-indulgence, and it has all been immense fun but he's perhaps now somewhat sated with idleness or ambitious of variety. He has sufficient means of his own, but the big augmentation of them depends, after all, on his mother and her business. The money he stands to earn there is really substantial. There is a certain element of the plastic and the wavering in him, but he may—he probably will—go back and take up his chances and his life afresh after this romantic interlude in Europe. But he isn't in any hurry about it. Let Woollett wait. As to Mme. de Vionnet, she *has* been charming, and well worth his support. He is not, however, the person to shoulder the lifelong responsibility for her. His recent lively contribution toward establishing her daughter in life has repaid any and all "debts" to the woman. Mme. de Vionnet will have to accept what she *must* accept. That he has provided a *dot* for her daughter is to his credit; it's also finely indicative of his attitude of using money to "square" the consequences of his behavior, since he's spiritually too poor to be capable of moral conduct.

When Sarah Pocock arrives, the young man's sister, married and two years older than himself, she promptly delivers her mother's word to the young man: if he doesn't come home now he needn't, for material advantage, arrive later; and she puts in her plea on behalf of the business and the family, and of patriotism and propriety, and whatever else she can think of besides. She sounds "the note of home—which is the very best thing she can do . . . the natural one; the right one." Sarah is accompanied by her husband Jim, and also by Jim's younger sister, little Mamie Pocock, a pretty young lady of twenty-two. Mrs. Newsome and Mrs. Pocock have hatched it between them that one aid to Chad's recovery may be possibly just this putting in his path of the little Pocock girl. It's quite characteristic of their confusions and misconceptions, or their complacencies and provincial standards of value, to have produced in Paris to stand in opposition to a brilliant and subtle woman of thirty-eight a necessarily so imperfectly accomplished, a so much less formed and less finished girl of sixteen years less—and to have done so for Chad's benefit, deliberately to attract his notice to contrasts. You see, at Woollett they are so *proud* of the little Pocock.

Mamie comes over with *her* idea of Chad, one manufactured in Woollett. She has formed an image of a fellow throwing up his business prospects for the sake of clinging at all costs to the women he loves. The woman, however, is attached only to his money. She's a heartless bad one, unworthy of him and of the sacrifices he is making for her. So Mamie has crossed the sea with her brother and his wife to save Chad from this foolish but noble infatuation. On the spot she sees a different picture and her castle crumbles. The romance of Mme. de Vionnet and Chad turns out disconcertingly other than what she was all prepared for, the general opposite of the image she was primed and wound up to deal with. It *isn't* the woman in this affair that's rather heartless, or more "practical" and colder. Her beguiled dream of rescuing Chad from the sacrifice of his career to love and to moral honesty evaporates. Mamie doesn't like Chad.

Jim Pocock has his explanation of Strether's behavior. Strether himself divines this and remarks it, but without recognizing its truth:

He wouldn't have expected it of me; but men of my age, at Woollett—and especially the least likely ones—have been noted as liable to strange outbreaks, belated, uncanny clutches at the unusual, the ideal. It's an effect that a lifetime of Woollett has quite been observed as having; and I thus give it to you, in Jim's view, for what it's worth. Now his wife and his mother-in-law have, as in honor bound, no patience with such phenomena, late or early—which puts Jim, as against his relatives, on the other side.

Mrs. Pocock's tolerance of such a state is of the shortest and her antipathy the liveliest, as is Mrs. Newsome's far away in the blue haze of distance. But Jim's own response to Paris is another variant of the type of Strether's and Chad's. His taste is lower, the quality of his amusements and pleasures inferior: in him the thing *is* open and blatant, coarse and crass and common; he is a simpler example of the spirit of the place practicing a sharp and more or less insidious spell upon the spirit of the person. The commonplace mind, the manners, the conversation, allusions, ideals, general atmosphere of Pocock constitute a humorous caricature of the attitude. He views the city away from home primarily as a field for amatory adventure with fast and loose hussies, liaisons with wicked sirens, for the indulgence of sex of a transient, an irregular and irresponsible, wayward and fleeting sort, a faithless sort with faithless women. Strether, Chad, and Pocock are all expressions of the idea of this: they display this likeness and appetite in three different ways, but Strether's is the superior case.

Sarah Pocock is represented as a much lesser Mrs. Newsome:

> Mrs. Newsome was much handsomer, and while Sarah inclined to the massive, her mother had, at an age, still the girdle of a maid; the latter's chin, also, was rather short than long, and her smile, by good fortune, much more, oh ever so much more, mercifully vague. Strether had seen Mrs. Newsome reserved; he had literally heard her silent; though he had never known her disagreeable. It was the case with Mrs. Pocock that he had known *her* disagreeable, even though he had never known her not affable. She had forms of affability that were in a high degree affirmative; nothing, for instance, had ever been more striking than that she was affable to Jim.

Chad of course treats Sarah and Jim and Mamie to his unfailing aplomb and his perfectly mannered geniality. He's light and easy in mood with them, cheerful, serene, indifferent, poised, affable, carefree—the reverse of compunctious or contrite over what he had done and had been, what he is doing and will do. He's the reverse of a man in any dilemma.

He was neither excited nor depressed; was easy and acute and deliberate—unhurried, unflurried, unworried.

He takes himself at the valuation put upon him by Strether. It agrees with his own self-appreciation. It coincides with and reinforces his own concept of himself and his general elevated view of his conduct and "talent for life." The young man's reply to his sister, and through her to his mother, is that in respect to his consenting to do what appears to them all so imperative and immediately urgent at home he will leave that to Strether, will abide by what his friend now says, and his own idea is that, if they can bring themselves to do so, his relatives shall have, while they're here, a good time.

Sarah had never sat with a countess before, but now a specimen of the class, the woman who has "made" Chad, or who is at least most responsible for his accession of polish and his admirable ease and courtesy, comes forward bravely, with her inexhaustible potentiality for being agreeable, and prepared infinitely to conciliate, to try to ingratiate herself with the rich and guileless, the strenuous and superior Americans from Woollett. Mme. de Vionnet, in it all, is magnificent; Mme. de Vionnet is wonderful; but these things are no more than what she is throughout. Both she and Chad, emboldened by their success with Strether, extend to Sarah Pocock *her* chance to be delighted with them. The daughter of Mrs. Newsome, however, is immune—unravished and unbedazzled. The inferior spiritual potential of the pair scarce makes them worth Mrs. Pocock's writing home about; their natures are too poor to have moral interest. She hasn't come over to congratulate either of the two on their behavior. The tune to which she is not delighted leaves Mme. de Vionnet on that side nothing to hope.

MRS. POCOCK: Do you consider her even an apology for a decent woman?

STRETHER: She has struck me from the first as wonderful. I've been thinking too, moreover, that, after all, she would probably have represented even for yourself something rather new and rather good.

MRS. POCOCK: Rather new? I hope so with all my heart?

STRETHER: I mean that she might have affected you by her exquisite amiability—a real revelation, it has seemed to myself; her high rarity, her distinction of every sort.

MRS. POCOCK: A "revelation"—to me: I've to come to such a woman for a revelation? You talk to me about "distinction" —you, you who've had your privilege?—when the most distinguished woman we shall either of us have seen in this world sits there insulted, in her loneliness, by your incredible comparison!

STRECHER: Does your mother herself make the point that she sits insulted?

MRS. POCOCK: She has confided to my judgment and my tenderness the expression of her personal sense of everything, and the assertion of her personal dignity.

Chad has passed to his sister his word of honor that he will let Strether absolutely answer for him.

MRS. POCOCK: He'll go in a moment if you give him the word—he assures me on his honor he'll do that.

If Chad goes back, he does so under Strether's influence; and if he doesn't, that too will be because of the push of Strether's weight upon him.

He habitually left things to others, as Strether was so well aware, and it in fact came over our friend in these meditations that there had been as yet no such vivid illustration of his famous knowing how to live.

Strether is not afraid of this burden of choice. He doesn't want it taken off him. He much rather doubles up his "forelegs in the manner of the camel when he gets down on his knees to make his back convenient." He doesn't want to have it to say to himself afterward that he hadn't courage for it.

There has been no change in his inward tone; the cause that has most driven him in this affair is still operative. He's in a situation in which damage was some time ago discounted. His "moral position" that keeps him up is precisely that there is nothing in it for himself.

Everything came back to Chad's knowing how to live.

> Strether 'surrendered himself accordingly, to so approved a gift; for what was the meaning of the facility but that others *did* surrender themselves? He didn't want, luckily, to prevent Chad from living; but he was aware that even if he had he would himself have thoroughly gone to pieces. It was in truth essentially by bringing down his personal life to a function all subsidiary to the young man's own that he held together.

James here suggests the essence of what is wrong with Chad's life in Europe. He is living selfishly, for his own pleasure purely, and one doesn't go to pot or fall to pieces only when one is of some use: when one lives to some extent also for others, and when one keeps hold of some sense of social responsibilities.

The Pococks linger only briefly in Paris. They leave that precious city for Switzerland for a planned stay of a month's duration, at the expiration of which time they will surely embark for home.

> SARAH: We've many things to think of at home, and great responsibilities and occupations, and our home is not an impossible place.

Strether, by their action, is granted a last delay—he has asked for one—in which to reconsider and make up his mind; and he is, by the turn of Mrs. Pocock's screw, so to speak, moved nearer to the crux of his case. The woman, in Switzerland, awaits his supreme reply. She prays it will take the form of a final beneficent interposition with Chad; and not that he will advise something that will be a further aggravation of Chad's case. She has of course signified abundantly that she regards the direction of Chad's development as hideous and also that Strether's own strange laxities and perversities and general surrender to the enemy she considers the reverse of edifying. Chad may have a sufficiency of material riches, he may be well enough off *economically*, but with Mme. de Vionnet he will have no proper wife, no children, and no work to occupy him.

The ultimate vacuity and futility of a life without work is to be remembered. Civilization, if Strether speaks of that, is founded upon effort of various kinds, not upon voluptuous languorousness. The interests and occupations of Chad seem the reverse of arduous, and it is thinkable that in time he will have doubts himself about the value of what he is doing, will become sated and bored by leisure, and guilt-ridden by the consciousness of not doing *something*. As to civilization and culture again, it is a matter of attitude quite as much as of opportunity, is essentially and decisively a matter of inner factors, of the form and substance of the vessel carried to the fountain no less than of the water supply itself, and nothing is more indispensable to it than a large spiritual capacity. The *good* life, the only one that isn't on the whole a "sell," involves the enlargement of one's spirit, the letting of one's *soul* live. The highest culture is moral taste. And so far as ethical sensitivity or opacity be a question of environment, it is near Mrs. Newsome, his distinguished mother, that a sound basic morality is more likely to become somewhat more his compass and helm for living. Moreover, it is the lad's mother that can assign Chad to his proper place in society, one in which his special and marketable talents can be exercised. And when he is in Woollett she will then be in a position to exert some leverage upon him. In Woollett Chad might conceivably undergo some moral regeneration, a place not unfriendly to this process.

The affair of Mme. de Vionnet and Chad is continued only by the debasement of both their characters, and Mrs. Pocock's opinion of this is simple and sharp. The Frenchwoman ranges herself, to Sarah's vision, in the category of those vampirish women who destroy a man's work and life. Wherein does it so greatly concern Strether about *this* woman, and to what does she consider herself entitled from him, or, for that matter, from Chad? Mme. de Vionnet has no claim on Chad, and the young man's total circumstance is such that to refuse to jettison her on grounds of morality is at best to do a little justice only in terms of a greater injustice. Strether's mind seems as one led captive by some charm or spell. The bad woman has got hold of *him* too in Paris somehow, and uses him for her own fell purposes, to his moral and material ruin.

Some time after the departure of the Pococks, Strether goes off on a little solitary midsummer excursion in the country outside Paris, a place where people come out from the city to boat, to dine, to dance, to make love, to do anything they like; and there he is suddenly placed at the heart of his subject. He comes unexpectedly upon Mme. de Vionnet and Chad together amid a cluster of signs of intimacy presented in a way it is impossible to blink. With all allowance for his demonstrated singular obtuseness of making believe to his own mind, his consent to be beguiled by thin speciousnesses, this encounter is unambiguous, is full of informing and convincing things for Strether. It tells him what he had previously shirked from puzzling out for himself, and he has to drop of a sudden from the golden dream of the "virtuous attachment" as a fallacy too fondly, too blindly entertained. He had dispossessed himself of the faculty of seeing things as they were but the quantity of make-believe involved is now too great. The old gentleman's sublimest presumtion is controverted, his bubble pricked: Chad is proved, perversely, not a Platonist after all.

The truth of Chad's relation with Mme. de Vionnet at last is markedly apparent even to Strether: the pair are intimate with the last intimacy. It was perhaps partly the process known as giving the benefit of the doubt, refusing to reflect meanly on Chad's spirit, and on Mme. de Vionnet's, as something to be imputed or presumed without proof. Widely enough, then, opens the chasm between the assumed, as Strether had taken it, and the attested, as he has now to take it. When offered as a supposition, what he has now to take wouldn't have "done" for Strether at all, in relation to other inward matters. He had averted his head, but the reality came out and cleared the air nevertheless, and with that occurrence the woman is quite at the center of her situation with the old gentleman. She sends for Strether the next day to see what the moral difference thus made for him might amount to; whether or not the administration to his consciousness of the supposedly clarifying dose, and its truly quite humiliating correction of his fatuous illusion, as he must now view it, has resulted in a revulsion in favor of "the principles of Woollett." With Chad solicited by Woollett, restless, precarious in her hands, she fears any shock that will send Strether swinging back to Mrs. Newsome and bringing the young man with him. And Mme. de Vionnet does have an interest in the decent appearance, if not in the reality itself, at least where Strether is concerned. As James forecast in his "project" of the novel, Strether's last conversation with Mme. de Vionnet is

> probably the most beautiful and interesting morsel in the book, and I would say most handsomely "done"—say so did I admit that there can be any *difference* of morsels in any self-respecting work-of-art, where the morsel *not* handsomely done simply incurs one's own pity long before the critic—if there *were* a critic!—has cut the eyeteeth of any knowledge of *how* competently to kick it. You must leave me accordingly with this passage and with my treatment of it. It is really the climax—for all it can be made to give and to do, for the force with which it may illustrate and illuminate the subject—toward which the action marches straight from the first.

In it James shows what he needs to show. Strether hadn't hitherto properly and logically compelled Mme. de Vionnet to commit herself to whatever of disadvantage the situation she had got into might throw up, and she has been intelligent enough to see this behavior as necessarily rooted in affection. But she has taken advantage of this affection as a special weakness in him. She has *used* him, knowing he has a persuasive influence with Chad, to keep the young man for her, and she requires his patronage and support still, which are but other names for a false position. Mme. de Vionnet, pre-

cisely like some woman less clever and less rare, is fearful and
in depressed spirits over the possible loss of Chad and another
matter. The young man has become a cherished "necessity"
to her. She ignominiously clings to the youth even though he
does not with any intensity return her emotion, and to keep
him near her she would have him cast away his material
future and spoil all his other prospects. The difference between unselfish love and an undisciplined lust is clear, and
the real stuff of which she is made appears. The quality of
her emotion for the fundamentally inconstant and superficial
young man, under stress of which she has let Strether ruin his
own prospects in its service, simplifies and abases her, presents her as a case. Morally she is of comparatively small
account, and the glory somewhat fades from her even to
Strether's vision. Her interest is still undeniable, but it has
lost some of its fineness of quality. The possessive passion
toward the loved object she represents and the possibilities
of wrongdoing for its gratification she betrays strikes him as
a sorry state. It is not a pleasant picture. She has a revulsion
herself, and is touched and moved to gratitude by Strether's
having pronounced her "all right." Moreover, Mrs. Newsome
has not been the only woman agreeably and favorably affected
by Strether. So also has Mme. de Vionnet, in her degree, and
she lets him know this so that he can make of it what he will.

MME. DE VIONNET: Selfish and vulgar—that's what I must
seem to you. You've done everything for me, and here I am
as if I were asking for more. But it isn't because I'm afraid—
though I *am* of course afraid, as a woman in my position
always is. I mean it isn't because one lives in terror—it isn't
because of *that* one is selfish, for I'm ready to give you my
word tonight that I don't care; don't care what still may
happen and what I may lose. I don't ask you to raise your
little finger for me again, nor do I wish so much as to mention
to you what we've talked of before, either my danger or my
safety, or his mother, or his sister, or the girl he may marry,
or the fortune he may make, or miss, or the right or the
wrong, of any kind, he may do. If after the help one has had
from you one can't either take care of one's self or simply

hold one's tongue, one must renounce all claim to be an object of interest. It's in the name of what I *do* care about that I've tried still to keep hold of you. How can I be indifferent to how I appear to you? Why, if you're going, *need* you, after all? Is it impossible you should stay on—so that one mayn't lose you?

STRETHER: Impossible I should live with you here instead of going home?

MME. DE VIONNET: Not "with" us, if you object to that, but near enough to us, somewhere, for us to see you—well, when we feel we *must* . . . Where *is* your "home"; moreover, now—what has become of it? I've made a change in your life, I know I have; I've upset everything in your mind as well: in your sense of—what shall I call it?—all the decencies and possibilities. It gives me a kind of detestation . . . What I hate is myself—when I think that one has to take so much, to be happy, out of the lives of others, and that one isn't happy even then. One does it to cheat one's self and to stop one's mouth—but that is only, at the best, for a little. The wretched self is always there, always making one somehow a fresh anxiety. What it comes to is that it's not, that it's never, a happiness, any happiness at all, to *take*. The only safe thing is to give. It's what plays you least false. You know so, at least, where you are! . . . I don't really pretend I believe you couldn't, for yourself, not have done what you have. I don't pretend you feel yourself victimized, for this evidently is the way you live, and it's what—we're agreed—is the best way. . . . You'd do everything for us but be mixed up with us— which is a statement you can easily answer to the advantage of your own manners. You can say "What's the use of talking of things that at the best are impossible?" What *is*, of course, the use? It's only my little madness. You'd talk if you were tormented. And I don't mean now about *him*. Oh, for him—! You don't care what I think of you; but I happen to care what you think of me. And what you *might*. What you perhaps even did . . . we've thrust on you appearances that you've had to see and that have therefore made your obligation. Ugly or beautiful—it doesn't matter what we call them—you were getting on without them, and that's where we're detestable.

We bore you—that's where we are. And we may well—for what we cost you. All you can do *now* is not to think at all. And I who should have liked to seem to you—well, sublime!

STRETHER: You're wonderful!

MME. DE VIONNET: I'm old and abject and hideous. Abject above all. Or old above all. It's when one's old that it's worst. I don't care what becomes of it—let what *will*; there it is. It's a doom—I know it; you can't see it more than I do myself. Things have to happen as they will. Of course you wouldn't, even if possible, and no matter what may happen to you, be near us. But think of me, think of me—!

STRETHER: There's something I believe I can still do.

MME. DE VIONNET: That won't help you. There's nothing to help you.

STRETHER: Well, it may help *you*.

MME. DE VIONNET: There's not a grain of certainty in my future; for the only certainty is that I shall be the loser in the end.

STRETHER: That's cheerful for your benefactor!

MME. DE VIONNET: What's cheerful for me is that we might, you and I, have been friends. That's it—that's it. You see how, as I say, I want everything. I've wanted you too.

STRETHER: Ah, but you've *had* me!

The tragic vanity of all that has happened is brought out for each, in Strether's last scene with Mme. de Vionnet, and this marks the dramatic climax of the situation. Glimmering through a mist of other things is still her passion and fear of losing her *young* lover, and Strether is still open to *that* solicitation, serves her in that to the end. He doesn't back down from his decision; he has been staggered and he has to brace himself afresh, but he becomes still more admonitory in the sense in which he has already positively advised Chad. That's only the climax of his original feeling and shows the full measure of his attachment. With the extent and kind of intimacy and domesticity, as now more fully disclosed, less than ever would it be honest or kind of the fellow to leave Mme. de Vionnet in the lurch. One can't brutally cast the compromised woman aside like a used garment. Besides, he holds that Chad, by meeting his mother's wish, will lose more than he will profit. As between Mme. de Vionnet and Paris versus Woollett and the advertising department, he still decides for Mme. de Vionnet. Let the publicity racket go; that is what *he* would do. Paris still meets his conception of the agreeable. The place is as much as ever the aesthetic antidote to the ugliness of the rest of the world, an education of the taste, a revelation of new sources both of solitary and of social joy, and a better field for experiment in living, a more intelligent climate in which to circulate, the opposite of narrow, humorless, intolerant, earnest, intense. He is as much as ever attuned to the life of the city of blighting new lights and invidious shattering comparisons with Woollett. Style of a particular kind, when so highly developed, seems to leave no room for other quite contradictious kinds. Yet Paris is various enough to give one absolutely everything one asks. He still judges it quite the least stupid course for the young man to remain in Europe and with Mme. de Vionnet. The youth will be well advised to embrace them both and have the intelligence to get from them all that they have to give.

His view remains his view, and he frankly expresses himself to the fellow in that sense. He glosses over the losses to himself of these words, which is the last thing that he conceives Chad as being touched by, or for that matter, with any intensity, conceives Mme. de Vionnet. He is not disposed to weave *that* fine fancy about the pair, but neither does he intend to let the mean motive of his own material future, his personal problem, prevent him from giving the youth this benefit, now that other fountains have flowed for him, of what he regards as superior insight—and what is doubtless thought in some other quarters to be ill-judged, morally-muddled meddling. It will cost him his own chance of financial ease in his old age, and it will cost him the love of the wonderful woman at home, so full of high qualities too, but he is willing to accept moral credit for these renunciations. Strether has set Chad the example of sacrifice for Mme. de Vionnet by giving up the woman *he* has been attached to. And of course the poor fatuous *Review* is also spoiled for any future favor from the lad's worthy mother. He has already, in Paris, had the opportunity of contrasting the contents of that publication against the literary *Revue des Deux Mondes*. Well, at least when he had bound it in green he had "known" what he was doing. How far, in such a short time, he had come from Woollett, and how much he had left by the way. But there is the question of what now he will go back to, whether it will be anything so good socially and professionally and personally. At least the note in him of the pursuit of one thing after another but nothing for very long is maintained.

Chad has available for each of these sequences the same unperturbed blandness and good cheer; an attitude, by a happy constitution, easy and natural to him. Nothing that has happened possesses the least power to ruffle his air of equanimity. He greets Strether genially, and remains pleasant and polite; meets him with his grand coolness exactly as he had always done; preserves his graciousness toward him as if absolutely nothing had occurred. It's a revelation to Chad to learn, from Mme. de Vionnet, that Strether had really put stock in the "virtuous attachment." He had been as nearly frank about the woman as he *could* be. He had never blurted out the truth to Strether, never answered inquiries honestly about their relation, but no deception was intended: He had merely left it to be reasonably inferred from its attendant outward and visible signs. He himself had inferred that there was no basic difference in thinking between them about this. He had never so caught this vision of Strether's attitude.

CHAD: I don't know what you've really thought, all along; I never did know—for anything, with you, seemed to be possible . . . After all, you understand. I spoke to you, originally, only as I *had* to speak. There's only one way—isn't there?— about such things. However, I see it's all right.

Chad had been discreet about not "telling on" a lady friend, and his friends had been discreet about not making "improper" disclosures about Chad. The whole romance of conscious delicacy in regard to disabusing Strether confined the old gentleman to knowing the relation only as a misinformed observer, by the indirectness of its play. And the quantity and variety of experience in this sort supposable in Strether's own past life that might have served to guide him is of the slightest.

The data weren't sufficiently given to him, and he didn't make them out for himself. Yet the error of supposing the relation to be something subtly other than a simple sexual liaison had been Strether's own, and nobody else's at all. But for the state of his emotions, the truth might have sprung of itself, as rudimentary, out of such appearances as were given off by the pair. His cognition had been colored by his feeling; his failure to penetrate the transparency was rooted in emotion; and emotion one should never fail to appreciate the primary significance of. It all consisted of an emotion, and by that intensity did it hang as bravely as possible together. He had deceived himself much more than others had deceived him. It had been his own private consent to be beguiled so that he could the more imaginatively and innocently misconceive. The inward perversity had converted to its use things vain and unintended.

After Strether has exhorted Chad in the strongest terms and for the last time to accept the duties of his relation with Mme. de Vionnet and to continue it as a responsible one, he feels that his work is done in Paris. He doesn't see how he can do more with the fellow than he has already done to promote the opposite of his original errand. He has done then with Chad and he feels that the young man is ready, on his side, to let him pass away. The fellow has just returned from a short stay in London.

A FRIEND (to Strether): And is it your idea that there was some other woman in London?

STRETHER: Yes. No. That is, I *have* no ideas. I'm afraid of them. I've done with them.

The list of Chad's sweethearts belongs quite to some other record. The "life" of Chad is wanton life—luxurious, licentious, unrestrained, unworried, roving, sportive, trifling. Any other sort he regards as appropriate only to the stiff, straight-laced people who don't live sensuously enough, the timid and inhibited who are afraid to let themselves go. He observes poor old Strether with the air of one looking down tolerantly, humoringly, from a higher level of life. Chad's intentions, qualifications, possibilities, or whatever else, in the connection, hadn't surely so much as the grace of the specious.

Through no fault of Strether's own, Chad will probably go back. He's at best only superficially a "culture-seeker," and the inducements of Woollett are much more tempting to himself than they are to Strether. Moreover, it's doubtful whether Chad has the inner resources for such living as Strether had imagined. So clear and strong a talent and character for advertising can scarcely be meant for finer things. The fellow will take the business on the side of the money to be earned by it, and he will doubtless exploit the thing capably as a source of large pecuniary profit. Strether has these past months acquired a greater personal knowledge of Chad, and his opinion as to what in respect to him is possible and not possible has altered. The revised Chad—the work of Mme. de Vionnet's hand, as Strether had been pleased to think it—is baser, however gilded, than he had supposed. Still it's an improvement of sorts over the prime version, as Strether remembers the raw youth. His thoughts are still uncomplicated by any strong moral feeling, there is some commonness in his mental predispositions, but the fellow has made a quick spring out of juvenility into elegance and smartness. On first acquaintance this acquired polish is what most immediately and iridescently shows. He has picked up the graces in Europe and from Mme. de Vionnet, if not the primary principles of conduct.

Strether, at any rate, himself will go back. He couldn't have gone before; the whole affair had become as a thing of his own that he had to watch and accompany out of a deep inward necessity or private perversity to its conclusion. He has had four months of experience and drama. He has been disappointed in some of the people, but he has had his sensations, impulse, passion, pleasure. The various contributive elements have all played for him toward a climax after which can only follow decline. He recognizes the conclusion of the affair, so far as *he* is concerned with it, when he sees it. Strether's late-coming to Paris—the journey for his health, for a change—has been worth while, he feels. It has worn the aspect of a runaway ending in a smash "fatal" to himself in its consequences, but Europe has also not failed to uplift Strether's spirit, has touched the chord that makes him most aptly vibrate. He has had experience in a range previously closed to him; and he has enjoyed himself in a way he hadn't done very much at home, and in a different mental atmosphere. The experience has represented something— meager and belated and indirect and absurd as it may be— that he has done for his poor old infatuated and imaginative self. He has lived by his own impressions and built on them, and he has received them of a kind in Paris as he had never in Woollett. Could one feel anything with such force without feeling it as an immense little act or event of life? An indigence has been relieved.

But before he goes back, after he has seen Chad and washed his hands of him, and after he has seen Mme. de Vionnet on corresponding lines, there is another person he is left face to face with. Strether is represented as attractive to women. Mrs. Newsome, we figure to ourselves, has in her time practically "proposed"; and recently Mme. de Vionnet has had a suggestion to make. Now Fate holds before Strether, before she has done with him, another chance to accept love. Miss Maria Gostrey has not been named hitherto, although she figures in the novel continually from its beginning as a friend to Strether. Or, as James puts it in his Preface, she is the reader's friend much rather: she engages Strether in talk, and his portrayed intercourse with her throws up to the surface what it concerns us to learn. She is an American expatriate, thirty-five and unmarried, left by the accidents of life free to wander, full of Europe, inordinately modern—the fruit of her international conditions, both highly unshockable and highly incorruptible. She has taken an extraordinary fancy to Strether, and at the very last she tries to go beyond her function of eliciting for us luminously the conditions in which he is involved; she shows him he can marry her on the morrow if he will.

Strether is all touched and intelligent about this, and he doesn't do anything so "vulgar" as to take it up. He *can't* assent. He doesn't return her love. It wouldn't be in accordance with the things that have come most to characterize him. But he *is* willing to go off with credit for this "renouncement" also: he lets poor convenient, amusing, unforgettable, impossible Gostrey have as his reason his "moral position," which he could more suitably address to Mme. de Vionnet—if to anybody at all. What has kept up his ethical sensibility throughout has been the thought that there is no ulterior personal advantage in the service of which he has been working against Mrs. Newsome. If he obtains anything—or anyone —this position weakens, for it may then be imputed that he has been acting in an interested way.

STRETHER: I must go . . . to be right.

MISS GOSTREY: To be right?

STRETHER: That, you see, is my only logic. Not, out of the whole affair, to have got anything for myself.

MISS GOSTREY: But, with your wonderful impressions, you'll have got a great deal.

STRETHER: A great deal. But nothing like *you*. It's you who would make me wrong!

MISS GOSTREY: But why should you be so dreadfully right?

STRETHER: That's the way that—if I must go—you yourself would be the first to want me. And I can't do anything else.

MISS GOSTREY: It isn't so much your being "right"—it's your horrible sharp eye for what makes you so.

STRETHER: Oh, but you're just as bad yourself. You can't resist me when I point that out.

MISS GOSTREY: I can't indeed resist you.

STRETHER: Then, there we are!

The subject of *The Ambassadors* is obviously, and quite as usual with James, the exhibition of a case, a state of feeling raised to intensity, swollen to voracity, and of some of the complications and personal consequences so begotten. The novelist allows nothing to obscure the clean definition of what he seeks to display, and there can be for him only one logic and one direction for his developments—the quarter in which his subject most completely expresses itself; and a subject residing in somebody's excited and concentrated feeling about something—both the something and the somebody being of course as important as possible—has more beauty to give out than under any other style of pressure. Intelligent consciousness, an honorable amount of it, in the person to whom the author most invites attention, is a necessity for interest. However, a particular kind of truth of resistance must also be imputed to the central figure; *some* intensity, some continuity of resistance is of the subject's essence. And successfully to resist the strain of observation and the assault of experience, what would that be, on the part of so aged a person as Strether, but to remain fresh, and still fresh, and to have even a freshness to communicate?

The center of our interest is in the consciousness of a good American who near the term of a prolonged life in a town of provincial size in the New England of the nineteenth century finds himself in presence of the "European" order without previous relation to it, a completely unacclimatized presence destitute of any element of preparedness except its immediate strong tug at his sensibility. The plan of the novel calls for "no end" of sensibility in Strether; he feels and vibrates to "Europe" with such an intensity as might be paid for by some corresponding lack on another side. Immensely moved by it as he is, he has so to deal with it. He is called upon for discriminations on foreign ground, in an alien social order, immediately subsequent to the first break in his ignorance, and with his freshness still predominant—a freshness that had become more so with the years and is now all accumulated and mature with having long waited for that advantage.

His business, as an observer, as he sees it, is to understand the life that surrounds him, the life that, while enjoying the sight of it so, he feels so out of. He does not respond poorly; he meets things "halfway," with spirit and intelligence, receptive, appreciative, grateful, even with a possibly too abject acceptance of the new grand air; and the drama is the inner drama of that consciousness, its action goes forward within that mind. He feels enough to be interesting, and the novel is the record and mirror of his reaction to such a stimulus, the adventure of a fresh intelligence, a mind accessible to new impressions and perceptions of a certain high order, a mind fine enough to be capable of profiting, indeed even of being "bowled over" by all the civilization, all the accumulations that are put before him in Europe.

Coming from New England into a Parisian atmosphere of things, he is confronted with certain arrangements of life less intense about work and duty, and more thoughtful of pleasure; a social tone that does not equate pleasure with sin. The levels at which they move at Woollett are but two: the strenuously upper and the abandoned lower. He discovers also in Paris a state of civilization providing for the beauty and dignity of art, upon his arrival from some perfectly humane community with forms of intelligence that are yet all incapable of providing for this. The "artist" in Strether misses what the hardness and dryness of the New England soil or its icy ambient air don't affect him as containing, and "Europe" furnishes an outlet for other things in him that Woollett had cramped and repressed. His inner pressures are released.

The idea requires, to express itself, a set of relations, each of which illustrates its particular bearing on the theme. There is Mrs. Newsome, whose own sum of experience is more or less what Strether *had* known, and with whom he sheds his pretended faith as promptly as she proves herself so incapable of exorcising with him their own old standards and touchstones and of replacing them with the new perceptions that stand him in their stead. There is her son Chad, the boy he wishes to wisely counsel and befriend, whose seed, when transplanted to a richer soil, had sprouted and flowered, whose reaction to "Europe" is of a generic sameness to Strether's own, and with whom he sees a temperamental kinship in his preferences. And there is the woman to whom the springing of such fruit from Chad's seed he regards as a glorious tribute to her handiwork: such a presence as Mme. de Vionnet, whom he had come over to have as little to say to as possible, but who so deeply speaks to *him*. Events were to expose her to the imputation of a larger tolerance from him than she had intended to require, or than he had originally intended to extend; but he *does* finally rise to its extension, in no less, surely, than the just degree, since she *is* of the perfect felicity and better than aught else whatever, which is what she particularly liked to thank him for having believed.

The novelist's business, and the reader's, is to extract from Strether's current reaction—his extravagant advance with the corrective retreat yet to come—whatever it may be worth; and for that matter we recognize in him the highest exhibitional virtue. Strether is not only the extraordinary ironic center; he has the wonderful importance of lending to poor persons by the mere fact of their being involved with him and by the special scale he creates for them, a precious element of dignity and a virtue not in the least native to them. What he does by the richness and freshness of his imagination for appearances in themselves vulgar and empty enough qualifies him for the central position alone. He has simply to wonder about them and they begin to have meanings that they could scarce have hoped for.

The subject defines itself, in its superior interest, as not directly Chad's affair with Mme. de Vionnet but Strether's view and experience of the pair. Compared with Strether, Chad (for instance) would have been no use at all as the subject's sentient center, or offerable as a plate for impressions to play on. Thanks to the "value" represented by Strether, and to the position to which Chad is confined by that irradiation, the latter is at the best a "false" character: he is a *figure* behind which the author never goes; only Strether goes, a great deal, behind Chad, and James goes behind Strether. With the appointed *quality* of Strether's consciousness we can trust him not to betray, to cheapen, or, as we say, give away, any value or beauty in Chad and his relation. He is resolved not to impute meanly; he refuses to read vile meanings into possibly beautiful things; and under that dispensation he has to register the nature of the tie formed between the two. He brings to their affair a sense of their intimate affinity and congruity, and the reciprocity of their desire. He sees the consistency of this relation of Chad's with his other relations; its common congruity with the rest of his life.

The pair meet a want of Strether's decent imagination, and he lends their affair *his* value; he reads into it his high refinement. The image and the sense of Chad and Mme. de Vionnet and their affair we so get, the one that glimmers through Strether's own exhibitory vision of things, is thereby criticized by these higher standards. Our interest in Chad is chiefly where Strether didn't quite make him out, and if the expression of the old gentleman's state shows through this, the contrast also, incidentally, constitutes the straightest of judgments on the younger fellow. He does the relation really too much honor: his imagining is the case rich and edifying where the actuality is pretentious and vain.

Across the sea is the world of Strether's workaday life and of matter-of-course propriety, but here in "Europe" is the palmier world of his divination and envy. And here happens to be the golden youth more fortunate than himself in freedom and ease, in money and opportunity, in sublime activities and prodigious possibilities. The lad, once away from the heavy hand of Woollett, has already mastered, by the mere aid of his own native gaiety and sociability, and by Mme. de Vionnet's, such arts of intercourse as testify eminently to the growth of his "taste," his active, quickened sense of life. Chad and the people about him are acquainted, one can't fail of seeing, with a tradition of manners that is rich and urban and apparently native to this air. Marks of a social order have rubbed off upon the fellow to give him serenity and "quality." These things are evidently what Mme. de Vionnet usefully taught and what Chad intelligently learned.

The sophistications of the "cosmopolitan culture" of Parisian society make an atmosphere "tonic" to Strether in his state, an air in the properties of which he blooms and flourishes—recuperates from the long strain of difficultly living in Woollett. Part of the enormous pull of Paris to hard-working, plodding, exhausted Strether is the delightful ease with which the seed of a greater life will grow in its soil, on the basis of general rather than special culture. "Europe" is an aesthetic

banquet spread out in front of the poor starved New Englander, a beauty to which one has simply to intelligently open
one's eyes and bask in its light in order to enjoy and assimi-
late. Strether's vision draws much to feed on in Paris, and in
the open air of attenuated spring days he lounges, passive
to the surge of culture that breaks upon him in waves; and
indifferent to the cold eye of Woollett at the time they are
"biding" for Chad and himself. He observes Chad enjoying
his round of pleasure with a grand good conscience. The
fellow possesses ways of remaining unashamed. And Strether
himself can't think a life of tasteful enjoyment—a life of art
and enjoyment and taste—by a pair financially and aesthetically capable of it, immoral. Pleasures of a certain high sort
appear, rather, to one who has to feed on but shrinkage and
privation, enviable.

Strether begins to think of all he has missed and now
dreams of. He reconsiders how far his lofty moral sentiments
have served him practically in the life *he* has followed with
so little to show for it. Is work and duty the whole meaning
and end of our lives? Is it not possible without giving up
"the hightest thing" to abjure a fanatical and impractical
morality, one that is too self-denying and narrowing, too
joyless and unintelligent, and to renounce an ideal of work
and service to others so high that nothing but unhappiness
comes from trying to follow it? There is a powerful pull for
Strether in a kind of life in which one can do what one wants
to do, whatever on earth one likes to do; a life of a large
leisure with plenty of time for enjoyment and for the attain-
ment of a better intelligence. And for the development of
any aesthetic and historic consciousness worth mentioning
this is the society. One is toned in it, as from steeping in a
rich old medium. To be indifferent to the opportunity of
such a life, not to judge it as the one most remunerative in
lasting value, would be too stupid. Strether can't be enthusi-
astic about Woollett after experiencing Paris. More things
worth living for are in Paris, and what Paris has on the spot
to offer Chad has but to take straight up from the culture
that superabounds all round him. It is this city that satisfies
more of Chad's nature and interests, or the better part of his

whole. And he is getting the good of things with such a peculiar degree of *ease*. Let him, then, just go on in the admirable direction he seems most inclined to, and continue to do what he *likes* to do.

The sterner realities are all drugged by the sharp Parisian spell. "Europe" is what culture "looks like" at its ripest; the social attitudes and the personal styles of the people "around" Chad suggest what life is capable of at its fullest. Chad, too, is an exemplar of this fine range and order of life. The semblance is there from which to infer the substance. And the youth shines in the light of his friends' distinction. He's either that, or the lad's comparatively nothing at all: Strether is thrown back on this for an alternative. An existence of advertising as the youth's true vocation and the sordidness of the idea of the false-hearted lover are possibilities scarcely conceivable to Strether's kindly disposed mind, are defamations of a gratuitous meanness.

Strether meets the situation of the lad who is not producing nor pointedly preparing to produce by a reversal of values; weary and worn himself, he quite throws over the religion of *doing* for that of *being* as the superior point of view of a well-balanced mind. Chad is such a gentleman, whatever he may or may not do. A New England whose "cultural" side is comparatively still a void would fail to deal with Chad's individuality, would not satisfy the logic of his particular special case. Strether had come out as a missionary to convert and save Chad from a woman and for the business, ultimately for the saving of his soul—as his mother, with her strong theological cast, energetically conceives the enterprise. But when in visual presence of the phenomena themselves he finds Chad saved in a way that Woollett, judging complacently at a distance and on insufficient grounds, possesses no suspicion of. Chad is quite good enough as he is: it is rather Woollett that is not "good" enough for Chad, or for the youth he conceives or projects as of a like general strain to himself. And he resolves to face the young man's crisis with him and see it through without a lapse and at no matter what cost to himself or to Chad.

He supplants his original purpose with its opposite. He

deems it the very source of wise counsel to advise the exchange of a business career for the aesthetic life as a profession, or at least as an absorption. Chad, with his better luck pecuniarily than Strether's, and than most, can manage without the executive job with its cash value and the social position associated with it, a life of dull "respectability" in the well-to-do upper stratum of Woollett—manage for luxury, that is, with the mere indispensable amount of money otherwise provided for. This boon, by good fortune, he already has a sufficiency of. He is far from being in any material need. In favor of the better order superseding, he would have Chad let everything in Woollett slide, as he himself sets him an example of doing. Strether himself lets go, for instance, the high *Review* of his own that had put forth its leaves under Mrs. Newsome's anonymous auspices, but from which his aesthetic sense now recoils.

Strether's decisions are active symptoms and dramatic communications of his state. He has seen Chad as Chad would best please him by being, but that vision was afterward to yield to other lights, to larger revelations and extensions of knowledge forced upon him accidentally. His prolonged hanging off from true knowledge was only beguiling for a time. Against the background of Paris, to such an imagination and freshness and responsive sympathy as Strether's, could the trick play itself with cards of such pale pasteboard. No occasion had hitherto laid so effective a snare for his type and temper. Chad and Mme. de Vionnet, all innocently, were the most gilded and baited of traps for Strether's wandering feet; a sufficiently pathetic, tragic, comic, ironic personal state.

THE GOLDEN BOWL

WE SEE everyone and everything during the first half in the interest of the Prince being handed over to us; and in Volume Two we see the same persons and things again as the Princess's exhibitional charm determines the view. It *is* always the Prince and the Princess, and it *is* always, thank heaven, marriage. And these are the things, God grant, that it will always be. But if the marriage should come to pieces—!

Or ever the silver cord be loosed, or the golden bowl be broken

If anyone should *want* to smash it—! The novel is more than fifty years old and its plot is "well known"; yet, in common with other late work by James, it will bear still more and more going into.

The principal characters are four: a father, his daughter, and two others. The father is an American millionaire who has turned to the collection of art after coming out at the top in the business world. He is a widower with one child, his single near tie, the one affection and one duty deepest rooted in his life; there is an exceptional degree of attachment between the two—he peculiarly paternal, she passionately filial.

You must know *(Freud writes)* that the number of women who until late in life remain tenderly attached to father-objects, or indeed to their real fathers, is very large. We have made the most surprising discoveries about these women who display intense and prolonged father-fixations.

Maggie is an out-and-out case of father-fixation, an exceptionally fine and special one with so much to make her so.

111

Then she meets Amerigo, a young Italian, tall, heartbreakingly handsome, high-born, cultured, clever, genial, charming, irresistible—bringing them down, in short, on every side. He is poor but he has a high social position and name. He is attracted to the extremely pretty and intelligent young woman, grows to be in love with her; and of course there is no suggestion that he doesn't also like the wealth of the Ververs. Maggie sees in his attitude and his position and in the whole cluster of his attributes a distinction that would add to her situation socially were she to marry him. The father settles a handsome *dot* on his daughter (leaving himself also plenty to live on), the wedding is accomplished, and the young husband is housed in dignity and crowned with comfort. It is made clear that Maggie's liveliest emotion, however, continues to be her affection for her father; she shows this as more intense than any sentiment inspired by her husband. To use the nomenclature of Freud (rather than the way she would put it herself) she has remained in the Oedipus complex and is unable to withdraw sufficient love from her father to love anyone else.

Amerigo really works for acceptance by the Ververs. His father-in-law seems to him simply the best man he's ever seen in his life. Mr. Verver's accomplishments, moreover, argue special genius; he's clearly a case of that. The two men take to each other beautifully, and the young fellow accepts from the first his wife's idea of still keeping her admirable father fast in her life. Maggie continues to spend large parts of her time with Mr. Verver.

In due course a principino arrives.

It was of course an old story and a familiar idea that a beautiful baby could take its place as a new link between a wife and husband, but Maggie and her father had, with every ingenuity, converted the precious creature into a link between a mamma and a grandpapa.

The young prince had at the beginning wondered whether his father-in-law mightn't perhaps decide to initiate him into the whole question of how money comes to those who know *how* to make it, mightn't perhaps help him to achieve some business comprehension and some active association with the great mysterious world of affairs, the money world, in which this gentleman has been such a conqueror. But he has since had plenty of time to ponder his wedded condition and it is no longer vague in him that it is a matter not of anything in particular that he is expected to do, but rather of what he's expected to *be*.

Wondrous at such hours could seem the savour of the particular "treat," at his father-in-law's expense, that he more and more struck himself as enjoying. He had needed months and months to arrive at a full appreciation—he couldn't originally have given offhand a name to his deepest obligation; but by the time the name had flowered in his mind he was practically living at the ease guaranteed him. Mr. Verver then, in a word, took care of his relation to Maggie, as he took care, and apparently always would, of everything else. He relieved him of all anxiety about his married life in the same manner in which he relieved him on the score of his bank account. And as he performed the latter office by communicating with the bankers, so the former sprang as directly from his good understanding with his daughter. This understanding had, wonderfully—*that* was in high evidence—the same deep intimacy as the commercial, the financial association founded, far down, on a community of interest.

It was a "funny" situation (*the young man concludes*)— that is it was funny just as it stood. Their married life was in question, but the solution was, not less strikingly, before him. It was all right for himself, because Mr. Verver worked it so for Maggie's comfort; and it was all right for Maggie, because he worked it so for her husband's.

The Ververs, father and daughter, are represented as always containing for the Prince some element of the impenetrable. He likens their motives to a curtain—not to one making an intended and ominous blackness; rather to

a thickness of white air that was like a dazzling curtain of light, concealing as darkness conceals, yet of the color of milk or of snow.

But he is so attached to his wife that he really cares for her freedom, cares for her doing what on the whole she most wants to, as it comes by the operation, the evolution, so to say, of her clear preference. It's for the Ververs, he considers, to see things exactly as they wish, and it's for himself to take them as he finds them without trying to force his wife to an attitude for which he would have no use in her if it were not sincere.

Mr. Verver, however, since the marriage of his daughter, has been beset by ravening wolves who want to marry *him*. He is still youngish, only in his forties, and Maggie doesn't see why he shouldn't marry as happily as she has—marry some person who would keep off ravening women without being one herself in the vulgar way of the others, and who would know how to be otherwise socially helpful to him; some woman who would gild and decorate their situation further.

It was as if you couldn't be in the market when you were married to me (*Maggie explains to him*). Or rather as if I kept people off, innocently, by being married to you. Now that I'm married to some one else you're, as in consequence, married to nobody. Therefore you may be married to anybody, to everybody. People don't see why you shouldn't be married to *them*.

Mr. Verver does marry again, some two years after his daughter; and he takes the so important step explicitly *for* his daughter, to free her of all sense of responsibility toward him. He marries a young American woman of very much his daughter's age and a friend of hers from school days. Charlotte Stant is a perfectly *social* creature, and if not prettier than Maggie is perhaps cleverer; she knows more what she is about. She is the poor girl who wasn't meant to be one, formed as she is by her nature and experience to rise to big brilliant conditions, take them splendidly, do all justice to them. Charlotte and Amerigo are both personally remarkable, in a high degree, all round, as are also, for that matter, Mr. Verver and Maggie. The high personal values thus clustered James not only accepts but cherishes; that they are each the particular individual of the particular weight being of course of the essence of his *donnée*. They give him more for interest that way; he has no use for them in any other.

Two distinct households are set up in London, but the father doesn't lose the daughter nearly as much as he expected. A large allowance of his company is still of the first necessity to her. She comes over to see him whenever she can. She likes him best alone. And since it's the way he best likes her, Mrs. Verver arranges for that. Charlotte accepts her husband's attitude on the matter of his daughter, wholly defers to it. She sees herself as "placed" or relegated by it— and she "knows" her place. The essence of her spirit and attitude is similar to Amerigo's. They both recognize the supreme emotional importance of Mr. Verver to Maggie.

CHARLOTTE: I've simply to see the truth of the matter—see that Maggie thinks more, on the whole, of fathers than of husbands. And my situation is such that this becomes immediately, don't you understand? a thing I have to count with.

Amerigo and Charlotte, without complaining, make the best of the extraordinary situation; they must live *in* it and with it.

AMERIGO: They're extraordinarily happy.
CHARLOTTE: Beatifically.
AMERIGO: That's the great thing; so that it doesn't matter, really, that one doesn't understand. Besides, you do—enough.

They give the people they love the life they prefer. They don't incommode them by the egotism of *their* passions. In addition, they have on their consciences some sort of return for services rendered. Well accustomed to taking as they have become, is not here just their opportunity to take also, and without wailing, whatever inconveniences for themselves are resident in the situation? Their consideration, their improbable *goodness,* which makes so much of their value, thus works to help Maggie keep in existence the situation holding them all. And they are, every one of them, people who "observe the forms," who know what inferiority the opposite of doing so is so much an implication of. Say Mr. Verver had married a woman who would have made a hash of them!

The Ververs are presumably ignorant of the sentiment that Charlotte had once entertained for Amerigo. Nobody concerned has ever mentioned it. The brilliant and interesting young woman had been in love with him, but nothing came of it—nothing could come of it, Charlotte and he being such nonmonied individuals. They couldn't afford to marry each other and he bravely gave her up. It had taken them some little time to feel the impossibility and then to face it; they had met constantly, and not always publicly, the whole of one winter. It ended with Charlotte facing it by bolting to America. That was more than a year prior to his becoming acquainted with the prettiness of Maggie. In any case it's all over. And now, strangely, her marriage to Mr. Verver has brought the attractive creature near him again, thanks to the particular conditions, as she could never have remained either as a single woman or as the wife of a different man. To look after his father-in-law's wife at social functions while Maggie and Mr. Verver are off together somewhere almost seems to have become the first of his domestic duties.

Being thrust, systematically, with another woman, and a woman one happened, by the same token, exceedingly to like, and being so thrust that the theory of it seemed to publish one as idiotic or incapable—this was a predicament of which the dignity depended all on one's own handling. What was supremely grotesque, in fact, was the essential opposition of theories—as if a *galantuomo,* as *he* at least constitutionally conceived *galantuomini,* could do anything *but* blush to "go about" at such a rate with such a person as Mrs. Verver in a state of childlike innocence, the state of our primitive parents before the Fall.

There were situations that were ridiculous *(he reflects),* but that one couldn't yet help, as for instance when one's wife chose, in the most usual way, to make one so. Precisely here, however, was the difference; it had taken poor Maggie to invent a way so extremely unusual.

The unmonied young man who has married the heiress
may be taken, or mistaken, for pleasure-loving and indolent;
the handsome and debonair lover, genial and charming
always in his relations with women, may be taken, or mistaken, also as somewhat inconstant and cynical, morally
something less than magnificent. James does his share, dia-
bolically, consummately, to let his real characteristics be so
misread, superficially. Actually Amerigo *is*, profoundly, a
Prince; all his conduct expresses it. He is not, as a nature,
as a character, as a gentleman, in fine, below his remarkable
fortune; the exhibited proceedings of the whole first half
are conducive to that being shown—so making it "his" volume in the sense indicated. He is represented as a Roman
prince genuinely in love with his wife and, as the great proof
of his affection, consenting to remain in abeyance for her
convenience. His being so is part of the interest of the situation; is just of the core of the subject: without his being so
the *donée* wouldn't come off as it does.

Maggie, all the same, begins to doubt of him, begins to
think him perhaps capable of strange and unnatural things.
Her first misgivings have come four to five years after their
marriage. Hitherto, to doubt of his fidelity and to doubt of
Charlotte's friendship have seemed impossible to her. What
has she been doing but generously trusting him with Charlotte? What has her father been showing but his utter confidence in his son-in-law? and in situations that hold out a
maximum of opportunity and temptation. They have, her
father and she, been acting on the theory that such temptations, however enormous, can't operate; they have been taking for granted that there is no capacity in either Amerigo
or Charlotte for deviation from their honor. Suppose her
father, too, should begin to doubt! One can never be ideally
sure of anything. There are always possibilities. Lately her
husband and Charlotte have been alone too much together
rather than separately. Even if there should be nothing between the two, an *appearance* is created that is equivocal.
Would that strike her father as something to be looked at
straighter? If anything should give her father a shake would
not their present, precious, precarious equilibrium waver?

Maggie has a vision of what it would mean for herself if any alteration in Mr. Verver's consciousness should cause him to take more notice of the queer things in their life, and to begin to wonder whether he has too passively accepted the whole pleasant funny form their life has assumed, whether it is so certainly for the best. Her desire can only be to keep him unconscious that, peculiar, if he makes a point of it, as their situation is, there's anything in it all uncomfortable or disagreeable, anything morally the least out of the way. She has to keep touching the situation up to make it, each day, each month, look natural and normal to him.

> she's like an old woman who has taken to "painting" and who has to lay it on thicker, to carry it off with a greater audacity, with a greater impudence even, the older she grows . . . For from the moment the dear man should see it's all *rouge*—!

Maggie decides to go out more with Charlotte, and she makes overtures which Mrs. Verver meets with alacrity. During their jaunts she regularly finds that Amerigo, who had likewise only wanted a hint,

> had come either to sit with his father-in-law in the absence of the ladies, or to make, on his side, precisely some such display of the easy working of the family life as would represent the equivalent of her excursions with Charlotte.

Maggie "recognized by the end of a week that if she had been in a manner caught up her father had been not less so—with the effect of her husband's and his wife's closing in, together, round them, and of their all having suddenly begun, as a party of four, to lead a life gregarious, and from that reason almost hilarious, so far as the easy sound of it went, as never before."

Maggie thinks it might be pleasant if Amerigo and her father should wander off together on a journey for perhaps a month in early summer, instead of all four of them migrating as usual to Mr. Verver's house in the country; but at this her parent demurs.

The point he made was his lack of any eagerness to put time and space, on any such scale, between himself and his wife. He wasn't so unhappy with her—far from it

Maggie has the chill of perceiving that Charlotte has begun to succeed to insinuate herself into Mr. Verver's affections. It has not, naturally, been the miracle of a night: it has taken place gradually, quietly, easily under the soft persistent pressure of that charming person's assiduous appeal. What happens is that little by little, inevitably, Mr. Verver succumbs to the personal charm of the remarkable woman he has married and that this constitutes for his daughter a crisis, giving us our drama, the course of which from this point has its center in Maggie's inner state, to the presentation of which the chapters of the second half are devoted. The high dramatic value of the part played by Maggie from this point as, driven by her deep-seated passion, she uses such means as she can to try to restore the previous balance and regain possession of her father, takes over from the Prince and his anomalous situation the center of our interest as the liveliest element in the action. The consequences, the ravages, of her emotion are the very center of the subject and we see them most vividly by keeping closer, in Volume Two, to the Princess' own vision. We are put more in the presence of what she herself sees; her feelings about her own case, what she takes it for, form the psychological picture; but the other realities, the circumstances with which she is in muffled combat, are not the less distinctly before us by being looked at largely through this reflected manner—seen and felt by us with that rich indirectness. It is not now for Maggie a question of conjuring away and arranging the beauty of appearances to the end that her father should not doubt of Charlotte and Amerigo—a comparatively simple matter! Her own doubts about the two have of late taken such definite and serious form.

Maggie takes in the first consciousness of *malaise* in her situation with her husband from signs of a possibly merely specious character. She has increasing suspicions; there are impressions that thicken and harden for her; but she hasn't at first any definite light. In time, however, she comes up against a sign that is conclusive for her, under which her sense of ambiguity totally collapses; one that gives her his delinquency not just as a subjective, possibly erroneous vision but in a full and lucid way. And she is at the same time— though this she is unable to admit—feeling the hold that Charlotte is gaining upon her father's affections.

For being first introduced to the Italian that became her husband Maggie has had to thank her clever friend Mrs. Assingham. The good Fanny's own youth and beauty now being largely of the past, one of this woman's present ways of living is to put her friends into relation with each other, and she had efficiently assisted this charming Italian to discover his Americans. The marriage of Mr. Verver to Charlotte had been another of her little ideas. The dear woman had somehow, from the early time, had a hand in *all* their fortunes. With her cleverness, competence, soundness, she has been an influence on them all, advisory, understanding, suggestive. And when Maggie obtains proof of the rightness of her suspicion, and her affair has been gathered ready to break, it is upon this person's intelligence and sympathy that she decides to throw the matter. She communicates nothing of it to her father nor to Charlotte.

Maggie has more and more felt that it hasn't been, since her marriage, just she and Amerigo at all, but she and Amerigo and Charlotte. Now, in consequence of remarks let fall by a shopman upon her purchase of a gilded crystal flask, she sees how things have been with the two *precedent* to her marriage. It has come to her that Amerigo's relation of intimacy started with Charlotte before Maggie ever met him, and it has come to her that the two went about together *after* Amerigo became engaged to Maggie. They were together all the while, up to the very eve of his marriage, not to speak of how they have been since that great event.

There is a great deal more to be said, the elder woman feels, than Maggie seems so much as able to want to understand. Taking into her hands the object that the girl considers to be an embodied evidence of a perpetrated wrong and the possession of which has been thereby poisoned for

her, Mrs. Assingham smashes the bowl. When Amerigo comes
into the room immediately thereafter, Maggie confronts him
alone over the fragments, and the scene that ensues brings
us up to the high point, the great *coup* of the action.

MAGGIE: It's the golden bowl, you know, that you saw at
the little antiquario's in Bloomsbury, so long ago—when you
went there with Charlotte, when you spent those hours
with her, unknown to me, a day or two before our marriage.
It was shown you both, but you didn't take it; you left it
for me, and I came upon it, extraordinarily, through happening to go into the same shop on Monday last; in walking
home, in prowling about to pick up some small old thing
for father's birthday, after my visit to the museum, my
appointment there with Mr. Crichton, of which I told you.

AMERIGO: You're apparently drawing immense conclusions
from very small matters. Won't you perhaps feel, in fairness,
that you're striking out, triumphing, or whatever I may
call it, rather too easily—feel it when I perfectly admit that
your smashed cup there does come back to me? I frankly
confess, now, to the occasion, and to having wished not
to speak of it to you at the time. We took two or three hours
together, by arrangement; it *was* on the eve of my marriage
—at the moment you say. But that put it on the eve of yours
too, my dear—which was directly the point. It was desired to
find for you, at the eleventh hour, some small wedding-present
—a hunt, for something worth giving you, and yet possible
from other points of view as well, in which it seemed I could
be of use. You were naturally not to be told—precisely because it was all *for* you. We went forth and we looked; we
rummaged about and, as I remember we called it, we
prowled; then it was that, as I freely recognize, we came
upon that crystal cup—which I'm bound to say, upon my
honor, I think it rather a pity Fanny Assingham, from whatever good motive, should have treated so. It was at a little shop
in Bloomsbury—I think I could go to the place now. The
man understood Italian, I remember; he wanted awfully to
work off his bowl. But I didn't believe in it, and we didn't
take it.

MAGGIE: Oh, you left it for me. But what did you take?

AMERIGO: Nothing, I think—at that place.

MAGGIE: What did you take then at any other? What did you get me—since that was your aim and end—for a wedding-gift?

AMERIGO: You received then nothing at all?

MAGGIE: Nothing but an apology for empty hands and empty pockets; which was made me—as if it mattered a mite! —ever so frankly, ever so beautifully and touchingly.

AMERIGO: Ah, of course, you couldn't have minded! But I don't make out, you see, what case against me you rest—

MAGGIE: On everything I'm telling you? Why, the whole case—the case of your having for so long successfully deceived me. The idea of your finding something for me—charming as that would have been—was what had least to do with your taking a morning together at that moment. What had really to do with it was that you *had* to; you couldn't not, from the moment you were again face to face. And the reason of that was that there had been so much between you before— before *I* came between you at all.

AMERIGO: You've never been more sacred to me than you were at that hour—unless perhaps you've become so at this one.

MAGGIE: Oh, the thing I've known best of all is that you've never wanted, together, to offend us. You've wanted quite intensely not to, and the precautions you've had to take for it have been for a long time one of the strongest of my impressions. That, I think, is the way I've best known.

AMERIGO: Known?

MAGGIE: Known. Known that you were older friends, and so much more intimate ones, than I had any reason to suppose when we married. Known there were things that hadn't been told me—and that gave their meaning, little by little, to other things that were before me.

AMERIGO: Then does any one else know? Any one, I mean, but Fanny Assingham.

MAGGIE: I should have supposed you had had by this time particular means of learning. I don't see why you ask me.

AMERIGO: I know nothing but what you tell me.

MAGGIE: Then I've told you all I intended. Find out the rest—!

AMERIGO: Find it out—?
MAGGIE: Find out for yourself!

As to Charlotte offering Maggie on her wedding simply her good wishes as a friend, if these were given in all sincerity and good faith, as we see they were by seeing Charlotte as we do, these good wishes imply the full renunciation of her own passion for the man whom she had lost in any case. In Charlotte's situation that was the only thing of value for her to have done; the thing that was wise and right. No material object is "in it" with the attitude indicated, even if there did exist some small piece of artistry at once cheap enough and yet having a charm.

The dramatic exchange between the wife and husband (in this sketch much abbreviated) is of course momentous for them both. It makes a sort of clearing up to "realities" between the two, leaves things not as they were, leaves Amerigo a bit staggered as to what it involves for him, wishing so, as he does, to keep well with Maggie. He has now to reckon with its coming out for her that he had known of old so much more than he had ever said, and he measures the rate at which equivocal appearances, as interpreted by his wife, have been supporting her case against him. On the other hand, the unexpected piece of plausibility or implausibility, depending on the point of view, that Amerigo has been able to put forth so impromptu when confronted with the evidence of his wife's discovery of him with Charlotte just before his marriage gives Maggie something to ponder. What he has told her about the circumstances lets her see that the bowl isn't altogether the ideally objective determinant of a high degree of guilt she had confidently taken it for and acted upon. It isn't at all a thing she could take to her father and smash both of their marriages with. She had considered that it represented something by which she could hold the guilty pair in her hand and make them do what she likes, from fear that otherwise the news of their misconduct would reach Mr. Verver's ear. As evidence it had looked like solid gold and it was as such she had used it to precipitate developments. Now it is before her as horribly possible that she had acted under a delusion. Her whole idea may have a crack in it. There wouldn't be any terror for them if they have nothing to hide. Maggie, then, has the horror of finding good seated, all at its ease, where she had only dreamed of evil.

She had made her husband his scene precisely that as a result of it he should confer with the sharer of his guilt but Amerigo decidedly doesn't go to Charlotte over the question of what Mr. Verver "knows." He lets Charlotte alone, and Maggie sees that he does.

MAGGIE (*to Mrs. Assingham*): He hasn't let her know that I know—and, clearly, doesn't mean to. He has made up his mind he'll say nothing about it. Therefore, as she's quite unable to arrive at the knowledge by herself, she has no idea how much I'm really in possession. She believes, and, so far as her own conviction goes, she *knows,* that I'm not in possession of anything. And that, somehow, for my own help seems to me immense.

Immense. For what she has to fear now is anything that would determine her father's wife to take Mr. Verver

into her confidence as she couldn't possibly as yet have done, to prepare for him a statement of her wrong, to lay before him the infamy of what she was apparently suspected of.

It would show her as sufficiently believing in her grasp of her husband to be able to assure herself that, with his daughter thrown on the defensive, with Maggie's cause and Maggie's word, in fine, against her own, it wasn't Maggie's that would most certainly carry the day.

Charlotte is now for Mr. Verver's daughter like some dangerous creature that has escaped from a cage. She has

her vision of the gilt bars bent, of the door of the cage forced open from within and the creature imprisoned roaming at large.

Maggie *tries* to observe the forms of serenity in the face of this change in her life but her emotion is too strong for her to be able to stomach any real continuance of relations with her father's wife in the way now prescribed to her.

CHARLOTTE: Have you any ground of complaint of me? Is there any wrong you consider I've done you? I feel at last that I've a right to ask you.

MAGGIE: What makes you want to ask it?

CHARLOTTE: My natural desire to know. You've done that, for so long, little justice.

MAGGIE: For so long? You mean you've thought—?

CHARLOTTE: I mean, my dear, that I've seen. I've seen, week after week, that *you* seemed to be thinking—of something that perplexed or worried you. Is it anything for which I'm in any degree responsible?

MAGGIE: What in the world *should* it be?

CHARLOTTE: Ah, that's not for me to imagine, and I should be very sorry to have to try to say: I'm aware of no point whatever at which I may have failed you; nor of any at which I may have failed any one in whom I can suppose you sufficiently interested to care. If I've been guilty of some fault I've committed it all unconsciously, and am only anxious to hear from you honestly about it. But if I've been mistaken as to what I speak of—the difference, more and more marked, as I've thought, in all your manner to me—why, obviously, so much the better. No form of correction received from you could give me greater satisfaction.

MAGGIE: "If" you've been mistaken, you say? You *have* been mistaken.

CHARLOTTE: You're perfectly sure it's *all* my mistake?

MAGGIE: All I can say is that you've received a false impression.

CHARLOTTE: Ah then—so much the better! From the moment I *had* received it I knew I must sooner or later speak of it—for that, you see, is, systematically, my way. And now you make me glad I've spoken. I thank you very much.

MAGGIE: I've affected you evidently—quite accidentally—in

some way of which I've been all unaware. I've not felt at any time that you've wronged me.

Maggie's desire is not to make things any worse for herself than they essentially now have to be. To break with Charlotte would mean to lose sight of her father altogether, to lose touch of him, cease to have to do with him at all, which is not to be thought of. But the full cup of her happiness is broken. That is to say,

> it was only the golden bowl as Maggie herself knew it that had been broken. The breakage stood not for any wrought discomposure among the triumphant three—it stood merely for the dire deformity of her attitude toward them.

His wife's lying to Charlotte gives Amerigo the clue and sets him the example; he takes his line from her, accommodates himself to it. When Mrs. Verver, in snatched opportunities of conference, asks him if he knows what is wrong he puts the haunted creature off with false explanations, maintains the contrary, insistently lies.

Things grow more tense. The effort of pretending carried on from week to week, to look and talk and move as if nothing in life were the matter, becomes more and more of a strain. "They learned fairly to live in the perfunctory; they remained in it as many hours of the day as might be." Amerigo snatches at pretexts for absence from Fawns in the August days. He is arranging books in his residence in the city.

> he had gone to London for the day and the night—a necessity that now frequently rose for him and that he had more than once suffered to operate during the presence of guests, successions of pretty women, the theory of his fond interest in whom had been publicly cultivated.

He goes also to escape the sight of his wife's smothered anguish.

Maggie is doomed to lose her father completely through wanting him all too much. She foresees this, and in her extremity of dread of it, to try what last she can to prevent the separation, she goes to Charlotte. In a passage of drama the two, for the first and last time, give up pretending. Charlotte plans to take her husband to America—and not to wait.

CHARLOTTE: Oh, I know my difficulty!

MAGGIE: Do you mean *I'm* your difficulty?

CHARLOTTE: You and he together—since it's always with you that I've had to see him. But it's a difficulty that I'm facing, if you wish to know; that I've already faced; that I propose to myself to surmount. The struggle with it—none too pleasant—hasn't been for me, as you may imagine, in itself charming; I've felt in it at times, if I must tell you, all too great and too strange, an ugliness. Yet I believe it may succeed.

MAGGIE: You want to take my father *from* me?

CHARLOTTE: I want really to possess him. I happen also to feel that he's worth it.

MAGGIE: Oh—worth it!

CHARLOTTE: You've thought *you've* known what he's worth?

MAGGIE: Indeed then, my dear, I have—as I believe I still do.

CHARLOTTE: How I see that you loathed our marriage!

MAGGIE: Do you *ask* me?

CHARLOTTE: "Ask" you? Do I need? How I see that you've worked against me!

MAGGIE: Oh, oh, oh!

CHARLOTTE: You haven't worked against me?

MAGGIE: What does it matter—if I've failed?

CHARLOTTE: You recognise then that you've failed?

MAGGIE: I've failed!

The last part occurs in the London house to which Maggie and Amerigo, in the more or less torrid August, have come back. Charlotte sends a telegram that she and Mr. Verver will take tea with them before sailing.

AMERIGO: Why don't they at least come to dine?

MAGGIE: That we must certainly ask them. It will be easy for you. But of course they're immensely taken—!

AMERIGO: So immensely taken that they can't—that your father can't—give you his last evening in England?

MAGGIE: Perhaps it's for the fancy, after all, of their keeping their last night in London for each other.

AMERIGO: But it isn't—is it?—as if they were leaving each other?

MAGGIE: They have their reasons—many things to think of; how can one tell? But there's always, also, the chance of his proposing to me that *we* shall have our last hours together; I mean that he and I shall. He may wish to take me off to dine with him somewhere alone—and to do it in memory of old days. I mean the *real* old days; before my grand husband was invented and, much more, before his grand wife was: the wonderful times of his first great interest in what he has since done, his first great plans and opportunities, discoveries and bargains. The way we've sat together late, ever so late, in foreign restaurants, which he used to like; the way that, in every city in Europe, we've stayed on and on, with our elbows on the table and most of the lights put out, to talk over things he had that day seen or heard of or made his offer for, the things he had secured or refused or lost! There were places he took me to—you wouldn't believe!—for often he could only have left me with servants. If he should carry me off with him tonight, for old sake's sake, to the Earl's court exhibition, it will be a little—just a very, very little—like our young adventures. In that case he will leave you Charlotte to take care of in our absence. You'll have to carry *her* off somewhere for your last evening; unless you prefer to spend it with her here. I shall then see that you dine, that you have everything, quite beautifully. You'll be able to do as you like.

Her father, the pearl of parents, is dying for her. Not physically; he's far from having done with life. But dying for *her;* and making her feel it by the fact of there being so much of him left—for others.

AMERIGO: But will you do still one thing more for me? . . . Wait.

MAGGIE: Till they've left the country?

AMERIGO: Till we've ceased to see them—for as long as God may grant! Till we're really alone.

Mr. and Mrs. Verver come to tea, but they do not stay to dinner.

Maggie is represented all through as unconscious of the real reason behind what she does, and what we see largely is how it appears to her own consciousness and condition. What James is up to, as usual, is the depiction of rationalization, directly and vividly; the disease of consciousness that permits evil to mask and parade in the guise of good. He contrasts the real things of the spirit against the apprehended superficial and specious construction of them. What makes a James novel the spiritual adventure it is is much less a matter of the objective and impersonal "facts of the case" than the accompanying prodigiously subjective side of the experience. Maggie beguiles herself. She finds herself attaching her fancy to "the so possible identity of her father's motive and principle with her own" and she dissimulates to herself Mr. Verver's decision to go back to America with his wife as motivated by his wish to save his daughter's marriage by removing the temptation of Charlotte from Amerigo. He married for her and he is doing this for her also. She blinds her eyes from seeing that her father really cares for Charlotte. The marriage bond between them she pictures as a "twisted silken rope."

> the likeness of their connection would not have been wrongly figured if he had been thought of as holding in one of his pocketed hands the end of a long silken halter looped round her beautiful neck. He didn't twitch it, yet it was there; he didn't drag her, but she came.

After the Ververs depart and Amerigo has attended them to their carriage, while waiting for her husband's return Maggie has a moment of suspense as to what attitude he will take toward her.

> she had an instant of the terror that, when there has been suspense, always precedes, on the part of the creature to be paid, the certification of the amount.

She is soon relieved by him, and it is on this note that the thing closes.

> MAGGIE: Isn't she too splendid?
> AMERIGO: Oh, splendid!
> MAGGIE: That's our help, you see.
> AMERIGO: "See"? I see nothing but *you*.

And the truth of it had, with this force, after a moment, so strangely lighted his eyes that, as for pity and dread of them, she buried her own in his breast.

THE IVORY TOWER

JAMES was born to write novels, to write them without strain from the beginning to the end of his days, and to write them ever better and better out of a constantly enriched natural capacity. His aptitude for learning was extraordinary, his mind susceptible of improving itself step by step indefinitely. He advanced in life and in his art; his vision kept altering with age and he could not therefore write his old stories and novels again, nor any more like them, but he could always compose new ones of deeper wisdom and ever increasing technical accomplishment with the same astonishing rapidity; and to treat oneself to so great an intellectual adventure as to read through his work chronologically—a literary output that is of the largest—is to note a perpetual outgrowing of stages and phases, an artistic evolution that culminated only in the very "last words" left incomplete by his death.

His precious latest then, *The Ivory Tower* and *The Sense of the Past*, what we have of them—they exist only as fragments, although large enough to have been issued post-humously in volumes of about 350 pages apiece—are the last supreme steps in the evolution of a great novelist: they are what James had come to finally after a lifetime of experience and practice, an uninterrupted growth in craft and wisdom; proof that although he had for some years been enjoying a great late period, so fruity an autumn surpassing all of his previous seasons in value, he had at seventy not yet exhausted his capacity for innovation and was still continuing to improve his quality, to refine further his literary methods and thought, both his spiritual and stylistic progression. What could his genius do except grow and grow?

One does not, however, wish to exaggerate. James did not after all flower into a single supreme final felicity that supersedes all his rest. He enjoyed many years of intense creative activity and accomplished sublime work in large amounts: and it is with the impressiveness of his achievements in their total mass that he may best enter the gates of greatness. The last fine tracings of his pen in essence are refinements of the ideas, the techniques, and the style he had previously brought to extreme advancement: they do not in any marked degree differ from his other late novels. The point is simply that his beautiful intelligence had not passed its prime even in its last employments, and that although he was the reverse of having been cut off before he could reach fulfilment he did nevertheless die, in old age, with his full genius for expression still in bloom, his useful life and his great work unfinished, and while still splendidly using for the purpose of mature and masterly art the very latest of his time. He maintained a ripeness of intellect without falling into any decay. His high joy in questions of life and love, of loss and gain, continued unabated; he became an even greater master of his words; and for force and felicity he drew upon increasingly larger resources of imagery and symbolism.

Continuous growth is the sign of all artists of the first rank, and there is in *The Ivory Tower* then, to consider here only this product of his fullness of time, although there would be an equal amount to say for the other, not only an absence of imperfections consequent to technical inexperience but no falling off of mental fertility. Despite all his past development there is here still some fresh invention and some increased linguistic vitality applied to the same originality of method, the same daring and delicate technical construction he had made peculiarly his own.

That the chief practitioner of the novel did not live to make his few final points and to complete the last refinements of his approaches to final form is a loss to literature, but enough, luckily, was written and projected in notes to give their measure and even to embolden one to attempt an abstract of *The Ivory Tower's* plot. Rather, there is the characteristic duality of plot which took some genius to manage, the false seeming that is the screen or camouflage for the real action taking place behind its cover, all wrought and conveyed with such admirable subtlety that it is still his virtually unknown achievement. The peculiar character and excellence of his powers at the time of his later writing is bound up with the double vision that increasingly grew upon him with age. It is in the plenitude of this quality that he is indeed great and so startlingly special.

Let us look into the characters of *The Ivory Tower* and their story on both of its planes. There are four principals: Gray and Horty, the two young men; and Rosanna and Cissy, the two girls. There are also two old financiers, Abel Gaw and Frank Betterman, who die and leave their fortunes to Rosanna and Gray. The novel deals with the effects of this inheritance. The characters and settings are American.

Rosanna Gaw, thirty-four years old, tall and fat, plain and quiet, is the marriage catch of her set, being the only child of a father who is possessed of twenty millions of dollars. The other girl, Cecilia Foy, is extremely social in temperament and very pretty, but poor. The two young men are also without much money, but one of them is related to Frank Betterman.

Betterman lost his wife early and also his two children and did not marry again. Gray is his nephew, the son of his half-sister and a man named Fielder. Betterman had had a business difference of a rancorous kind with Fielder and the marriage of his half-sister to this man to whom he had such a strong objection dissociated him rather thoroughy from her. Fielder, however, soon died leaving his young wife and small boy with scant means, and also disconnected now from her rich brother. She betook herself with the boy to Europe and after no long time engaged herself to an Englishman, a fellow also of no great means but this time a person with whom Betterman has never had any dealings.

Betterman has never seen the new fiancé Mr. Northover. Nevertheless the general pattern of the proposed union is of a nature to displease him. The boy Gray will become a step-son by it, as Betterman himself became in his own youth by a second marriage of his father's which he hadn't at all liked. So Betterman sends word to his half-sister that he has learnt her intention and thinks very ill of it, but that if she will get

rid of her low foreigner and come back to America with the
boy he will forgive her and do for her what he can.

Mrs. Fielder's inclination is to stick to her honorable suitor
of whom she is very fond, and who is very much in love with
her and also likes the boy.

> She answered her brother that his demand of her was
> excessive in the absence of anything she could recognize
> that she owed him. To this he replied that she might marry
> then whom she liked, but that if she would give up her boy
> and send him home, where he would take charge of him
> and bring him up to prospects she would be a fool not to
> appreciate, there need be no more talk and she could lead
> her life as she perversely preferred.

This poses for Gray's mother a dilemma and she decides to
solve it by taking her fourteen year old son into her confidence. She puts it to the boy that, young as he is, *he* decide,
if he can, what they shall do.

Betterman in America during this period is immersed in
in a business association with Abel Gaw, and Mrs. Gaw and
her daughter Rosanna are abroad for "cultural advantages."
The partnership of Gaw and Betterman is already spotted
with irate disagreements and mutual recriminations of the
kind that such lives are plentifully bestrewn with and of
which the consummation was to be a violent rupture, but
nevertheless Mrs. Gaw and Rosanna have formed in Europe
the friendliest relation with Mrs. Fielder and Mr. Northover
and Gray, and take the liveliest sympathetic interest in their
question.

Rosanna, being sixteen, older by two years than Gray,
takes upon herself to strongly advise her young friend what
decision to make in the weighty matter that has been laid
upon his small shoulders. She likes Northover, thinks him
charming, and she hates Betterman—who, as she understands
or believes, is in some iniquitous business way swindling her
father. She is also much affected by the tastefully quiet and
modest expatriate life in Europe. She contrasts its opportunities for cultural education with the awful game of grab for

which she is sure Betterman proposes to train his young nephew.

Rosanna's words act upon Gray and settle his question for him, and in the aftertime the girl has always known and felt that they did. Mrs. Fielder marries Northover and lives with him and her son in great happiness to her death, some ten years later. Northover then, with whom Gray has become great friends, requires and appeals to his care and interest in a way that keeps the young man on and on in Europe till the stepfather's death takes place just previous to the time of the novel's opening.

The action of the novel begins at the point when Betterman in his last illness sends for Gray, by this time a man of thirty-two, to come to him in Newport. The foregoing episodes are referred to by the characters retrospectively, as fundamentals in their past. Rosanna's bitterness toward Betterman has diminshed with the passage of years and in the light of more knowledge of what her own prodigious parent's career has likewise been and meant. To her maturer sense their malodorous quarrel shows very scantly for the credit of either party. She has also had some compunction about depriving Gray of a large material advantage: neither Gray nor his stepfather have been at all well off financially.

So when Rosanna hears of Northover's death she gets at the sick Betterman and discovers that he will listen to her story about his nephew. She goes to work on him; she wakes up the old wretch from being as horrid as possible to the end, brings him round to doing some decent thing about Gray—who is about the only person nearly related to him that hasn't ever asked anything of him or greedily tried to snatch anything from him. His nehew, as she reminds him, even turned down an advantage proffered. Her conscious motive is to rectify the possible disservice for which the young man has had her to thank and make up the quantity she has cost him; and it is as a consequence of her appeal that Betterman sends for Gray and that Gray comes. He comes simply to avoid a possible ugliness in his not coming.

Gray is not in the least business-experienced or financially-minded; he's different, he's cultural-education centered, and all the better for it. His sensibilities strongly incline to the aesthetic and moral, he's familiar with the arts and languages, he's devoted to the play of taste *as* taste. The idea of dealing with great publics leaves him cold; society or the world offers no temptation to him. His material wants are few and small and he has not thought much about the cash-box: his interest has been for the finer profit, all the interest that isn't on the money: he's not money-minded and yet not a blatant ass.

Now, what the past has done for Betterman has made him ripe for just such an appeal as Gray makes. Face to face with the young man he observes that Rosanna is right about Gray's value, right about his intelligence and rectitude, his lack of materialism and selfishness and of any faint germ of the money sense.

> He had seen you in the great fact about you (*Rosanna tells him later*), that you are more out of it all, out of the air he has breathed all his life and that in these last years has more and more sickened him, than anyone else in the least belonging to him, that he could possibly put his hand on.

The stamp of money has been on the thoughts and doings of everyone with whom Betterman has been connected, but his nephew doesn't do things for himself or push himself forward competitively: that sort of vision is alien to his nature and tradition, and he stands off from it. He's not a hustler.

BETTERMAN: You utterly loathe and abhor the hustle! That's what I blissfully want of you.

GRAY: You ask of me the declaration—? But how can I *know*, don't you see?—when I *am* such a blank, when I've never had three cents' worth of business, as you say, to transact?

BETTERMAN: The people who don't loathe it are always finding it somehow to do, even if preposterously for the most part, and dishonestly. Your case is that you haven't a grain of the imagination of any such interest. If you *had* had it would have stirred in you that first time.

GRAY: Yes, I think my imagination, small scrap of a thing as it was, did work then somehow against you.

BETTERMAN: Which was exactly against business. I *was* business. I've *been* business and nothing else in the world. I'm business at this moment still—because I can't be anything else. I mean I've such a head for it. So don't think you can put it on me that I haven't thought out what I'm doing to good purpose. I do what I do but too abominably well.

To be able to leave an innocent like Gray all his dubiously-acquired wealth imparts to Betterman a moral glow in which he dies happily. The fortune that the young man comes in for is several hundred thousand: no monstrous mass of dollars by the New York measure but a tremendous lot from Gray's point of view, in relation to his experience and needs; a quantity really, with his inexperience and inexpertness in mercenary matters, his utterly unbusinesslike, unfinancial type which has seemed most to decide his uncle that he should be the one to have it, that he feels himself totally unfit not only properly to use but even rudimentarily to care for.

Gray has a friend Horton Vint, a man of the street and market who lives in the air of business and breathes business easily and naturally, although he has not yet succeeded in gathering any rich pecuniary harvest of his own. Horty (pronounced Haughty) has pulled Graham out of a "fix" before, has done so physically in the Switzerland alps, in their earlier youth. Mr. Betterman's nephew and future heir had "strayed into a high place" but "slid down to a scrap of ledge, and so hung helpless over the void, unable to get back, in horror of staying and in greater horror of not." Horty, at no small risk of his life, had come to his aid and lowered him a rope by means of which he scrambled out of his exposed position, and this service has always since been present to Gray.

So Gray asks his former friend and rescuer who has a cleverness in the handling and investment of money to help him manage his financial affairs and relieve him of this burden for which his own competence is nil.

GRAY: I shall propose to you a percentage, if that's the right expression, on every blest benefit I get from you in the way of the sense of safety.

HORTON: You propose to me a handsome premium? Catch me not jumping at *that!*

GRAY: Yes, and you'll of course fix the premium yourself.

Horton is in a relation of moderate closeness with Cecilia Foy (Cissy), a young woman who moves in his set. She is intelligent and beautiful, they attract each other, there is an air of friendship between them, but they are not engaged. She is unmonied like himself and they have a similar attitude: they recognize frankly that in a world of money they can't afford not to go in for it, and that accordingly so long as neither has it they can't go in for each other. Horty's conviction is that in time he's going to have money but Cissy observes that somehow, engrossed in the pursuit of it as he is, and with all his affairs and ability, he isn't moving very far in the indicated direction. He doesn't seem to be the hard driving ruthless Betterman and Gaw type, and the methods he *has* used haven't apparently sufficed.

Horton indicates the difference between himself and Gray in some remarks he makes to Cissy.

HORTON: I remember he used really to exasperate me almost by seeming not to have wants, unless indeed it was by having only those that could be satisfied over there as a kind of matter of course and that were those I didn't myself have—in any degree at least that could make up for the non-satisfaction of my others. I suppose it amounted really to the fact that, being each without anything to speak of in our pockets, or then any prospect of anything, he accepted that because he happened to like most the pleasures that were not expensive. I on my side raged at my inability to meet or to cultivate expense—which seemed to me good and happy, quite the thing most worth while, as for that matter it still seems. *La lecture et la promenade,* which old Roulet, our *pasteur* at Neuchatel, used so to enjoin on us as the highest joys, really appealed to Gray, to all appearance, in the sense in which

Roulet regarded, or pretended to regard, them—once he could have pictures and music and talk, which meant of course pleasant people, thrown in. He could go in for such things on his means—ready as he was to do all his travelling on foot (I wanted as much then to do all mine on horseback) and to go to the opera or the play in the shilling seats when he couldn't go in the stalls. I loathed so everything *but* the stalls—the stalls everywhere in life—that if I couldn't have it that way I didn't care to have it at all.

It had been to the massively substantial attractions of Rosanna that Horty tried at first to commend himself, and all vainly. When he, some two years ago, had ventured to invite her to marry him she had turned him down with a finality and promptitude that have since remained to his memory as a model in their kind. Horton to Rosanna stands as the symbol of that danger against which she is most vigilantly on guard: the horror of being appreciated and approached only on the ground of her wealth. "Would any man ever look at her so for passion (*Rosanna wonders*) as Mr. Vint had looked for reason?" The physically unattractive rich girl is in the position of not being able to believe it possible that she can be loved for herself. This attitude, with the mistrusts and dreads it sets up, constitutes her character's and situation's deep note. Upon her father's death she has inherited twenty-two and a fraction of millions, a mountain beside Betterman's molehill; her father has wished to give her the benefit of the very largest attractions he could, and of the kind he most recognized; and she loathes every separate dollar of them.

Cissy takes an interest in Gray and is capable of understanding and entering into his tastes. She is the person around him with whom he discovers himself most able to communicate aesthetically and intellectually, much more so than with Rosanna. He doesn't at first see her as making up to him on account of his money: he has a horror of shrinking from relations with people from possibly groundless suspicions of that motive in them. He has nothing but terror of seeing himself affected as Rosanna has been by her situation and

she figures to him as a great warning light, a horrible example
of what to avoid. Nor does Rosanna intimate that Gray's
case need be at all like her own: she thinks her feelings right
and inevitable only for herself. But Gray observes that one
of the things that it means to have inherited, one of the boons
that his inheritance opens up to him, is this attractive and
sympathetic young woman, and he has some moments of
intoxication or exhilaration over the change in his conditions
before questions begin to come up that make a difference.

In the circle of business-minded and money-minded people
among whom Gray has now been set down his want of their
sort of comprehension and imagination is regarded as somewhat phenomenal, and to Gray himself his innocence of these
matters and his small natural aptitude for them are sources
of helpless shame. He has not at all at first a disgust for them.
For him business and finance have retained their mysterious
character, and he holds what he doesn't know somewhat in
awe, yet with certain reserves and reflections; and he is
dazzled, but with the same reserves, by the financial brain
of the friend to whom he has been glad to make over the
care of his new funds and properties.

Gray keeps himself disconnected from Horty's manipula-
tions with his fortune, nor does he permit any meddlesome
intervention by others. Being himself without the experience,
talent, or inclination to arrange his now large affairs, he gives
his friend a free hand to do this for him. Every monetary
question and decision is left to Horty's judgment. Everything
that Horty brings to him he signs, but only what Horty
brings. The fortunate heir thus keeps himself splendidly free
of business shackles in order to devote himself to those richer
treasures about which he is by nature and education competent, retains his life of uncommitted hours for the sake of
certain dispositions or inclinations that he has, in his own
way, deeply cared about and felt.

As the consequence of this full frankness of understanding
between the two men on the matter of Gray's inaptitudes
Horton exercises a large control over the inheritance, and
with this occurrence his own fortunes soon show a notable
growth. His connection with Gray (as he explains to his

friend) gives him a boost in the New York financial world
such as he has never before had and he is becoming with
remarkable rapidity a less and less nonmonied individual.
He is helping himself by helping Gray.

Cissy begins to see the improvement in Horty's finances,
and she likes to see it. She likes also to let him know that she
likes it. It is at last successful proceeding by Horty, the promise and propect of material acquisition on a big scale. Gray,
however, is drawing upon his own newly acquired income
with what might pass for the most extraordinary timorous-
ness. He is still as much as ever privately enlisted against
these things, the money passion being genuinely alien to his
nature, his wholly unfinancial type. He's both an out-and-out
nonproducer and a nonaccumulator of material gain. All
the attraction, to his dissimular vision, resides in an idea of
the quiet life and all the revulsion to his sensibility in the
mercenary stress and bustle. He does only the social things
that are prescribed for him as the least he can get by with
doing, mainly those that are foisted upon him as open to
him to do for his friends.

The kind of attraction that Cissy has for Gray is strong
enough to prompt him, before acting upon it, to directly ask
Horty what sentiment he has for the girl and to clarify the
kind of his tie with her.

GRAY: Do you mind telling me if it's true—what I've heard
a good deal affirmed—that there has been a question of an
engagement between you and Miss Foy—or that you are so
interested in her that to see somebody else making up to her
would be to you as a pang, an affront, a ground of contention
or challenge or whatever?

Horty says emphatically No, and Gray accepts his denial.
He *wants* to believe it, at the moment, in the interest of his
own freedom of action. But he later comes upon his friend
unmistakably "together" with Cissy under some particular
illuminating conditions. Horty, then, has merely given Gray
the answer that would most please him, and has done so
for the sake of keeping well with him. He *can*, it appears,

lie to him, and for Gray this discovery clears up a number of questions. It shows him how much Cissy is at present really thinking of Horty as well as he of her; and it shows that Horty now estimates his affairs to be going so well for him that he can consider the possibility of marriage. That is to say he can afford to marry someone other than Rosanna, no longer having need of her resources to make up for his own destitution. And Gray apprehends that Cissy keeps *two* men in her balance or on option, as it were, one rich and the other rapidly becoming so, to see what will come of them. He notes the effect on her of the money-making power in Horton. It gives him the pitch of her wants and ideals.

Other vivid illustrations of the force and prestige of money confront him all round in this society of ferocious acquisition. And he can't help but be struck by the vulgar uses to which rich people about him put resources that should enable them to do immense things. Hideously expensive architectural monstrosities have glared at him from right and left in Newport. Flashily shining jewelry and a huge possession of other conspicuous ornament have assaulted his eyes, not to speak of extravagances and enormities of expenditure of every other tasteless sort. The multiplying number of costly and complicated American mechanical contrivances as "aids" to this and that is new and foreign to him. The insistence on them, the way everyone among the lot appear aware of no values but those sets up its effect on his nerves.

His ignorance and indifference toward these overstrained accumulators of tangible substances having cash or market value gives way to some experience of contact with them, and as time passes he begins to acquire an apprehension of how so many of the "spoils" all round him are triumphantly come by. An impression takes form of the black and merciless methods that are behind the great—and for the most part queer and ugly—possessions, the wrongs in which they invariably seem to have their origin. What Gray has learnt about the history of his own money from people he has talked to who knew Betterman is hardly of a nature to soothe him. And he has had from Rosanna's lips her observation of what money had done to her father, the horrible result of Abel

Gaw's wishing to do with money on such a scale, how she had seen it dry up his life to everything else and make its meaning small.

ROSANNA: Having to do with it consists, you know, of the things you do *for* it—which are mostly very awful; and there are all kinds of consequences that they eventually have. You pay by these consequences for what you have done.

Gray feels himself too different—both too inexpert and too estranged—from what now surrounds him to melt into it, to sufficiently surrender and be assimilated by this way of life. To try to be like everyone else about him would involve being least fine and least true to himself, and this would be to go awry and end in disaster. He finds it impossible to do what they do: he hangs back and stands off from committing himself to their attitude. They seem full of the poison of money and of business affairs without a blest other idea, and he feels the irrelevance of their scale for the measurement of his own different values. He's a pure negation of these "American" values, with the enormous preponderance of money in their life, having affected himself.

The first wonderments then begin to glimmer upon Gray as to just what the character of Horty's present successful methods are, what Horty is really doing with the matters in his charge, and as to whether or no he shall try to find out. Horty never flinches from the theory that he is "looking out for" and "taking care," consummately, of his friend, and he is just as consummately arranging to *show* for so doing; but Gray is quite otherwise preoccupied than with the things that Horty can either give him or take from him and he finds himself ceasing to believe in the fellow in proportion as Cissy is beginning to believe.

Augusta and David Bradham, a wealthy couple prominent in the American "high society," strike up an acquaintance with Gray and soon Davey attempts to borrow money from him. The Bradham fortune, which is all the wife's, has had its foundation dilapidated by the ravages Gussie keeps making upon it: it presents a large front or a fair outward face but is a much undermined and precarious quantity. Davey asks for the confidential loan of some big lump, an amount that Gray answers he will have to "see about," in other words inquire of Horton whether he may have so much without confessing what he wants it for.

The requested number of dollars doesn't suit Horty, even after Gray has been up to this time so ascetic in his spending.

> It won't be convenient for you just now, and I must ask you really to take my word for it that you'd much better not make such a call, much better not distract from what I am in the act of doing for you such a sum.

Davey, upon being accommodated only to the third or some other fraction of his appeal and observing that Horty won't let Gray have more, makes some humorous insinuations about the rate at which the financial caretaker must be "cleaning out" his friend and employer. These insinuations Gray defends Horty against as best he can although he recognizes as well as Davey the slenderness of Horty's excuse. Gray privately regards any malversation of his funds contributory to Horty's enrichment as something to which the fellow is being greatly encouraged and tempted by Gray's special attitude and ignorances, and he regards such malpractice for the sake of "hauls" as a natural consequence of the nefarious "American" attitude in these matters.

Subsequent to this, Horty comes to Gray with something dreadful to make a clean breast of, so dreadful that it can only involve the essence of his honor and his reputation and his safety before the law. He has been guilty of some delinquency or some large and unwise irregularity that has resulted in a disastrous loss of much of Gray's money, and also on a smaller scale of his own. He of course pleads the matter not as a thing involving his own obliquity but as a result of having been "done" by others.

Gray has reserves about the genuineness of Horty's story of the money's loss. He suspects the thing to be some major appeal for relinquishment practiced upon his simplicity and his liability to believe that the particular betrayal has been inflicted exactly as described. He has conduced to the event himself by giving the fellow such a free hand and furnishing such large chances for "doing." He considers it more likely that his friend has for once succeeded, with his assistance, in making an exceptionally Big Haul. And this sense is confirmed for him by the circumstance that Cissy in a sort of *thereupon* manner "takes up" more with Horty instead of not doing so—as figures to Gray as discernible if Horty were himself really minus.

Gray shows his former rescuer in silence that he understands and accepts and condones the loss and on consideration will do nothing, inquire into nothing, put nothing to the test. He goes by his theory of a noble indifference to money. Its loss doesn't so immensely matter that he should investigate his friend for it, or denounce him, or—still more abhorrent—expose him to any legal process. He will instead go back to Europe on his previously sufficient financial basis and there live quietly on an income of an extreme New York deplorability. He has in any case been disturbed by the thought of retaining and "enjoying" the fruits of Betterman's swindles; he has a total disbelief in any privileges of which the source is not pure; he feels in his wrought-up condition that the ill-gotten gains carry their curse with them and that this is after all the most congruous way of his ceasing to be concerned with them and of resigning them to their natural associations. He withdraws from the set of people in which the misdeed has been perpetrated and from the whole miasmatic "American way of life" with its wild spending and its financial rapacity which leads to such cheapness and inversion of lives and values. He has had America, and America has "had" him. He removes himself from contact with its moral death to avoid contamination. Before he becomes himself infected by the hollowness and falsity of money-worship and commercial success he goes back with relief to his world of mind and spirit, of intellectual and aesthetic delights and moral rectitude.

This is Gray's own sense of the matter, which in the novel is of course immensely kept-up and done, but the real characteristics and exhibited proceedings of these people are quite other. Gray's private imputation of a remarkable baseness in his friend is a thing more of loose appearances than of sharp particulars. And although destitute of primary data Gray stops short and shuns the putting of his suspicions to a real and direct test by a sublime decision that it doesn't matter. That is, the establishment of Horty's true character doesn't matter. This enables us to get a bit into his truth. It is one thing to entertain no appeal to Horty or to project no redress against him and it is quite another to bear on one's "proofs" lightly and to cover this fact of holding off with the shallow ground of conscientiously "sparing" his former rescuer. This is a rationalizing psychology. Gray treats Horty to nothing but the very lightest and most delicate pressure because he is afraid that the desired presumption of the fellow's dishonesty will upon more and more inquiry emerge less and less clear: the deeper reason he abstains from the test of further development which so exposes the false and so consecrates the right is the fear of seeing himself rudely corrected. Gray is the last example in James of a failure of integrity in thinking, of the "criminal" or crooked use to which the intelligence may at a pinch be put of falsifying its history, forging its records, and appearing greater than the traceable grounds warrant.

We can, for instance, with a little good will easily conjecture that Horty, knowing Davey Bradham, has guessed the cause of Gray's unusually large and unexplained request and we then figure his denial of the full amount on some pretext or other as consonant with the fellow's theory of taking care of his eccentrically unfinancial friend. The dramatic climax was to be a scene in the eighth book between Gray and Rosanna, and the final two books in their picture parts were then all to be a matter of what appears to these two. They could scarcely be given over to the state of mind, the vision and feeling, of Horty. Gray was to have gone to Rosanna after the passage in which Horty confesses the big loss, somewhat staggered by the circumstance but still with some preserved uncertainty or darkness about it, and after a time with her he was to come away with the uncertainty dispelled and the remarkable light taking its place, a light having as little as possible of foundation in any additional dry data. Originally Gray had seen Rosanna as a danger to herself by her mistrusts of Horty and of inordinate wealth, but what the novel shows him succumbing to is this same poisoning of the mind that the young woman embodies in grosser form.

Gray is the only person Rosanna is sure of not regarding marriage as a method of adding something handsome to his income, and her love for him is the force that had set her in motion to work on Betterman. Rosanna, however, has no more aesthetic taste than an elephant; she is massive and magnificent only "morally," and it is to Cissy that Gray is attracted, not at all to the rich girl. There is in the depths of Gray's case the fact that he ceases to believe in Horty in proportion as he sees Cissy beginning to believe: that is, as the doing, the man of action quality in his friend, as to the show of which he had been previously so hampered, is given opportunity to come into play.

We have a company of characters in the novel and a picture of differences, and a variety of ways of being affected or haunted by money. There are of course Gaw and Betterman, latter-day Midases, men with a consummate special ability to make fabulously fast financial gains, who become bewitched by money's magic touch and resort to rather sharp practices. The degeneration, however, of men with a technical vision and small scruples who are engaged in a ruthless pursuit of wealth and who look at all human activities with an economic singleness of purpose, a vision that is culture-unconscious and blind to those values for which there is no mathematical attestation or no equivalent weight in gold, who think money to the point that prevents their estimating even themselves and other people but in terms of their "worth" in material possessions, is an interest contributive only to the greater one. The amusement, as material for fiction, in cold-blooded manipulators of men, schemers obsessed with money and power and who for the lust of it prey upon the stupidities and weaknesses and ignorances and helplessnesses of other people, letting their desires override their righteousness, is limited. The gross immoralities of gross people do not suffice to provide a high quality of interest, and James introduces more subtle and fresher and rarer types of misbehavior, artfully dissimulated but none the less kept in secret view. He gives the image and sense of the ravages of money-hunger while still keeping it subordinate to his main idea.

The characters and the set of relations are chosen to express a central idea which is effectually symbolized by the Ivory Tower, the sacred and solitary cultural refuge from the vulgarity of the world of affairs, and for the superior interest we are presented with no sensual or unscrupulous creature of prominent social position but instead with a small obscure person of sensitive nature or fine mind, special and exceptional and acute and interesting. Gray is not stupid nor coarse but endowed with intelligence—and yet befooled and bewildered. It is the *quality* of bewilderment characteristic of him that makes the finer comparative interest—that bewilderment without which there would be no question of an issue or of the fact of suspense, prime implications in any story.

Gray is a single illustrative case of the conflict between "culture" and "the world." We see that there *is* opposition, and why there *should* be is another matter. Now for art as a profession there need not be any difficulty about the things advantageously surrenderable, but Gray is represented as a dilettante in all the arts rather than as an active practitioner of any one of them. The trouble with him is a sort of excess of "culture" as the form taken by his existence up to the time of the novel's opening has both contributed to the growth of that article and detached him from any practical application of it.

The fellow is thirty-two years old, unmarried, and has always had a small regular income. He has no definite profession and has never had to hold a job, never had to manage an organization nor meet a payroll, never attend to the details and daily routine of any business, never to do any sort of work that is productive economically. He has never really had to accomplish anything specific within a set limit of time. He does not busy and embroil himself in those family and community and industrial affairs and cares with which adulthood is ordinarily concerned and he lacks that rounded experience which includes practical and fiscal considerations. He hasn't anything at all to show in financial gain nor in work achieved, good nor bad, but because he is possessed of a sensibility worth speaking of and has gone in so tremendously for cultural initiations he hasn't up to now had the sense of a vacuous consciousness or a wasted life either. His philosophic nature has turned him to the realm not of application but of appreciation and he has used his large leisure for study. He is covertly and waitingly and sceptically conscious of future possibilities of writing—which are, however, complicated by his fastidiousness.

He has been a recluse in the sense of a total absorption in his artistic talents haven't shown, apparently, for anything prodigious; but he has imagination and nerves and a fine organ of thought, he is extra-refined and ultra-perceptive, is without personal ambition and has a potentially fine nature. At the novel's opening, with the death of his mother and his stepfather, he has reached the end of his course in Europe: having already had a high degree of the advantage of a "European" education it is time for him to give a still finer twist to his life and to outgrow this stage he should now be ripe to shed.

He has been a recluse in the sense of a total absorption in "culture" and a neglect of undertaking those primary responsibilities of maturity represented by marriage and work. He has sustained an indifference to certain fundamental human values and he has abstained from contributing any share in bearing the communal burdens. Although he is gifted mentally he has been idle socially: his existence has been basically selfish and self-improving. "America" is the next logical term of Gray's progression and at this moment he is presented with a chance to realize exactly what he has been missing in life that is most important. With his array of purely intellectual and aesthetic resources and lack of any others here is the perfect opportunity to remedy what he

hadn't become and hadn't done and to realize life in more
of its fulness.

If he will keep his head, "America" is a golden chance for
Gray to supplement the subjective in which he is already so
rich with the objective, to emerge from his cultural education
and use it to participate in the problems of the world, to
unite his refined intellect and his refined sensuousness with
spirit. It is for the fellow clearly to grow bigger to meet this
occasion, and what else can he desire but to press forward and
embrace it in every way he can? In his first exchange of talk
with Horty after the big advantage has been thrust upon him
Gray indicates that he is not altogether unaware of its value.

HORTY: Do you mean, on your honor, that you don't *like*
what has happened to you?

GRAY: Of course I like it—that is of course I try to. I've
been trying here, day after day, as hard as ever a decent man
can have tried for anything; and yet I remain, don't you
see? a wretched little worm.

HORTY: Deary, deary me, that you should have to bring
up your appreciation of it from such depths! You go in for
it as you would for the electric light or the telephone, and
then find halfway that you can't stand the expense and want
the next-door man somehow to combine with you?

GRAY: That's exactly it, Vinty, and you're the next-door
man! I *can't* stand the expense, and yet I don't for a moment
deny I should immensely enjoy the convenience. I *want* to
like my luck. I want to go in for it, as you say, with every
inch of any such capacity as I have. And I want to believe in
my capacity; I want to work it up and develop it—I assure you
on my honor I do. I've lashed myself up into feeling that if
I don't I shall be a base creature, a worm of worms, as I say,
and fit only to be utterly ashamed. But that's where you come
in. You'll help me to develop. To develop my capacity I
mean.

HORTY: Your capacity—I see. Not so much your property
itself.

GRAY: Well what will my property be *except* my capacity?
It won't if I don't like it, that is if I don't *understand* it, don't

you see? enough to *make* it count. . . . But I come back to my point that it's you that I essentially most depend on.

The danger of going in for "culture" or anything else to excess and too exclusively is its tendency to carry one away from the earth up into the blue, away from *other* primary human concerns, from the voice of society, from the rest of life and all of its multiple and complicated affairs.

GRAY: It hasn't been to show you that I'm silly about life. . . . It has only been to show you that I'm silly about affairs.

HORTY: Well, what are affairs but life?

GRAY: You'll make me feel, no doubt, how much they are —which would be very good for me. Only life isn't affairs— that's *my* subtle distinction.

HORTY: I'm not sure, I'm not sure!

GRAY: Oh rot—*I* am!

What Gray is in want of is any genuine desire to serve. At bottom he's indifferent to the "America" of which he is so ignorant and he doesn't with any strength wish to learn all that's to be learnt about it in order to obtain a capacity to serve better. The appetite for aesthetic pleasure and the preference for refined intellectual passions are too strong in him for subordination to the life of a responsible citizen and he merely curses and dismisses "America" and goes back to "Europe," to a cloistered and barren erudition detached from life's central issues and neglectful of its deeper concerns. He reverts, that is, to his normal selfish self, dissociates himself from the business of living, and detours manhood instead of passing through it.

He decides to run out but in order to do so he has to explain this action in such a way as to make it creditable to his consciousness. He tries to make it appear to himself that it is his soul that revolts from the evil influence or corrupting power of the dollar-devil that these worldings worship and that he is abdicating a material kingdom and place of power in order to recover its spiritual equivalent and in order to continue to devote himself to "higher things" that more than compensate for his loss and to a less barbaric life. But this is a wisdom fair only to a superficial perception. Actually he is regressing morally and returning to the penalties that attend the drop of responsibility and the substituted rule of fatuity. In "Europe" he remains essentially a cultivated parasite on society, feeding his mind with intellectual and aesthetic acquisitions, continuing to give the widest berth to the spiritual fruit of social service, and not doing anything creative with his large freedom.

He is guilty of a subtle perversion of life rather than any strong debasement of it such as is the active pursuit of power and money immorally. He makes the capital mistake of enthroning "culture" as an idol in the place where spirit should reign supreme and is not himself innocent of a kind of rapacity, the very sin he is castigating. He is an extreme instance of the ravages of culture-hauntedness. He and the flagrant worldling Betterman are at opposite poles but they have in common selfishness, the gospel of self-indulgence, and the novel centered round their devastating contrast remains equivocal and double-edged. They move in different worlds, and these two worlds in which they circulate are both lower than the spiritual one of the pursuit of happiness through service—which is the greatest rightness of all and the really big life.

Betterman's thought in leaving Gray his fortune is that the young man imported from "Europe," by the mere fact of his presence and activity of spirit, will be a fresh and healthy counter-influence to the sparsity of cultural values in "America" and that by his incapacity for that deep subjection to pecuniary profit of the sort that Betterman recognizes in himself and his associates he will also set an example of a more moral life.

BETTERMAN: It's not for myself, it's not for myself—I mean your being as I say. What do I matter now except to have recognized it? No, Graham—it's in another connection. It's for the world.

GRAY: The world?

BETTERMAN: Well, our great public.

GRAY: Oh your great public—!

BETTERMAN: That's the way I like you to sound. It's the way she told me you *would*—I mean that would be natural to you. And it's precisely why—being the awful great public it is—we require the difference that you'll make. So you see you're for our people.

GRAY: I shall make a difference for your people—?

BETTERMAN: Don't think you know them yet, or what it's like over here at all. You may think so and feel you're prepared. But you don't know till you've had the whole thing up against you.

There are beautiful talents the exercise of which isn't lucrative and there are enterprises of much human value which are not financially or immediately profitable. And Gray has the sort of sensibility that opposes itself to just those elements in the "American" air that defeat the cultivation of the finer flowers—creatures of cultivation as the finer flowers essentially are. A person of his temperament and education has necessarily to fly in the face of everything in "America" that makes against culture: he will contribute in his own way by having a mind fine enough for restorative reaction against such things. He is most qualified, as Betterman thinks, to balance with "America" and to supply to its drama the precious element of contrast and antithesis. His immunity from the general infection makes him mysteriously and refreshingly different: a vessel of his essence is least likely to become soiled and stained by immersion in its workings and by contact with its materialisms and coarsenesses and its brutalities.

"America" is the great complex society that asks most from Gray's *whole* faculty, all to the bright advantage of his extension of view and his variation of activity. Betterman makes available to him a more eminent social position, one that will open up a range of experience previously closed and that will make him conscious of more things in the world, conscious of the world as something larger and more widely significant than "culture" in the sense of books and pictures and music and pleasant people and talk. The small intellectual appetite projects itself on few things but the big projects itself on many, interests itself in everything human.

Present to abundance in the air that Gray begins to breathe in "America" are just those elements he has lacked in "Europe," and also in the "American" air is a strong hostility to the growth of the very forms of excess to which the fellow is most prone and in need of correction—that is, of the pursuit of culture apart from its social value or human application to the primary affairs and relations of life. Gray is disregardful of the differences and suitabilities and values of others and inexperienced in dealing practically with people of various mental makeups and tastes; and he is out of touch with the ownership and management of things; he is detached from social realities and commercial considerations and utilitarian consequences. He has been too withdrawn from the conflicts of life; he has been separated from the makers and doers of society, the professionals who have had to *know how* to do something in the immediate field of life—which was to have learnt how, for action, for application, for getting through a job with all of its details and its frictions.

"America" is Gray's chance to get at persons whose history and talents have been determined in ways most different from his own. He has cared too little about economic questions and conditions, about the money-question, the money-vision, and of obtaining a grasp of the part played in the world by just these; "America" is his link with market realities and current social actualities. There are whole sides of life about which Gray has been largely ignorant and simply contemptuous and in which "America" is particularly strong. Here is his opportunity to enter into new relations and modulate into something different and better, to confront the world and fit himself for it. To make a sufficient response to America, to take root and grow in its soil, to let himself be nourished and conditioned by it, to involve himself in its practical and material affairs would be for Gray an extension of life, of experience and consciousness, a stretch in the direction of essential change, would be to make of his personal and social and professional life a fuller and deeper thing.

The people who make up the American society all about

Gray, according to their capabilities and their situations, are busily ministering to one another's needs and desires and this is the young man's opportunity not to shirk on one side or another a due share of the decreed burden but to make himself a useful member of this civilization. The influence of Gray and "America" upon each other should result in developments mutually beneficial. But what the novel shows him as doing is deplorably "muffing" this chance by any such employment of his time and talents. He but moons about superficially and circumferentially and displays a constitutional inaptitude and a base intolerance for accepting and carrying any such burden—repudiates any great moral or functional or useful character whatever. He remains at large and apart and unengaged in the tangle, an inactive and brooding "philosophic" spectator of life rather than its servant, free and uncommitted to the society that would draw him out of himself to something more widely significant, away from his own small questions to its own larger ones. But at the moment of financial crisis he exorcises as baleful the association from which he should derive great profit, demonstrates himself utterly unapt for any such valor as taking America without a pocket immoderately lined with gold, and while pretending magnanimity shows himself an ingrate to the steward of his fortune.

He runs away from the life, whatever it be, that surrounds and closes round him, the existing social life of his time and place, runs away from its knocks and bumps, from the friction of natural differences, from its inevitable ingredients of folly and vulgarity and boredom and stupidity, from the dishonesties incident in human affairs, from its problems and anxieties, its stresses and strains, from the weight of the burden of labor, from the intermingled delights and disconcertments of normal human adventures, from the terribly mixed-up world with its close connection of bliss and bale, of things that help with the things that hurt, from the love of life and the love of other persons and of many of the things of the world. This is his really swindled state.

The exploitation or victimization of Gray by some thoroughly corrupt creature would make for a less significant plot than the one that the novel bears in its main construction. Mere dense hardness and baseness, not wearing a mask nor feeling the need of one, was hardly James's strongest affinity in the matter of subject and the author has provided the fellow with a real situation that lifts the moral issue above such comparatively poor and stale interest as is obtained by common robbery. The person who ignominiously fails Gray at the supreme moment and who insidiously beguiles and betrays him for the sake of a personal and private interest is himself. The real betrayal comes from within, from the selfish and fearful forces that oppose one's finer promptings. Man's conscience is James's theme and states of moral illusion, rationalizing self-deceptions, the traps and tricks of thought, these inversions and reversals to be as artfully as possible communicated to the reader by their concrete representation, by vivid exhibition rather than flat statement. The more powerfully the element of portentous evil in "America" can be suggested the less ignoble and pusillanimous will appear Gray's decision to escape and fly away to his distant heaven of "spirit." The young man causes his situation therefore to positively reek with the air of evil, and to dwell on the "wrongs" done him while clinging to an ideal of his own faultlessness. Out of the depths of an unexplored sinister he succeeds in invoking the semblance of a victory, but it is without any substance. Spirit is spirit only as it is applied to the affairs of the world.

What he is then thrown back on is "Europe," reversion and regression to an ignobly peaceful and quiet and sterile existence isolated from life's deeper currents, and an air he has already breathed in such uninterrupted sufficiency. He will continue to abandon himself to the pursuit of a refined epicurean intellectual pleasure and let matters more fundamental languish. He will concern himself more and more with less and less. Living only for himself he will become increasingly ingrown, will remain a narrow and partial man void of connections with and into life at large. He will abuse by overuse the Ivory Tower, which is a holiday place and a temple for occasional quiet meditation, a place in which to pause from time to time to reorient or refresh oneself, by taking it for his permanent habitation.

So it is that he's depicted, with all the advantages of his own presentation of his case and according to James's notions of dramatic construction.

There is the existence merely gilded with money or with culture mistaken for the truly golden life: there is the false treasure supposed to be true and precious, and the real treasure supposed to be false and hollow. It is a significant fable. And the fine truth of the case, with its attached warning or lesson or morality, emerges sufficiently distinct notwithstanding its unfortunately unfinished state. In fact nothing could be more "done" in the light of its happiest inferential intention.

JAMES'S THEORY OF THE NOVEL

EACH OF James's novels is an improvement on the one before; he kept getting deeper into reality with the years; and as his vision of the truths and the subtleties of expression developed so did his vision become finer of the processes and mysteries of life, the moral and spiritual maze. His work, the whole large mass of it, taken in chronological sequence, is documentary of a rare and wonderful capacity for growth; from the array of his productions we may trace the foremost member of his craft through every phase of his career from its rudimentary stages to the extreme of maturity, the opening out of a great mind during a long life, the stretch of the years in which developments really take place, from example to example, from prodigy to prodigy, a store of mystery and meaning and beauty.

This is to say that the ideas which pervade and support the work of James increased in value, steadily and at an extraordinary rate, with the growth of his genius, and that the body of them, expressive of what he held most dear, a philosophy of art and of life, emerging at the time of his later writing, from the greater experience and the more powerful intelligence, ushered in his completely full and rich period, the years in which his genius most overflowed, the dear man's Indian summer and a very wonderful time. Having asserted so much it will be one's next purpose then, going in for greater braveries still, to convey one's sense of what a few of these ideas are—ideas of form, letting slide for the time, as another subject in itself, his ideas of life—from James's later vision, James at full growth as a conscious and consummate artist, ideas underlying and conditioning creative work of a ripeness, finality, and felicity on the highest plane of imaginative literature; work, in short, ineffably better than his early writings or even the novels of his mid-career, patently charming though we find them.

The novels that matter most, to his sense, are very packed productions, inclosing a good deal of one thing within another, and so resembling a shapely crystal box of compartments, springs, and tricks. They have some part sufficiently *within* some other part, sufficiently withdrawn and consecrated, not to constitute a thoroughfare. We see in them one thing *through* another and perhaps something else through that. They invoke every source of interest that they can, one after another finding its way in. The simple may enjoy them for their least bearing and the initiated for their greatest. The amusement is then at its maximum, by which term James always means the gathered cluster of all the *kinds* of interest. The aim is to make the novel bristle with as many vivid values, with as thick and yet as clear a little complexity of interest, as possible. The essential property of such novels is to repay effort on the part of the reader, to give out their finest and most numerous secrets, and to give them out most gratefully, under the closest pressure of the attention. They take for granted the public, or at the worst the not unthinkably private, exercise of penetration. They depend for being truly understood and enjoyed upon some responsive reach of critical perception, upon what, in such directions, we "go into" and how far we go. Appreciation is left very much to the mind capable of it and willing to do the work. The reader has, after all, not to create but simply to recognize with the last fineness.

In the novels to which we refer, those of the highest order, there is a central point at which the various implications of interest converge and interfuse to give the work its profound unity. Such a novel is comprehensively and richly *one*, its parts in abject dependence, all clinging together and pleading with a collective friendly voice; any great charm they may individually and capriciously put forth is infirm so far as it doesn't measurably contribute to a harmony. Its parts are all illustrations leaving us but half appreciative till we catch that one bright light in which they give out the best thing they contain. The "best thing" they contain is primarily an idea, a pursued and captured meaning, and the light of the consciousness of this idea is required for following the design of the work with intelligence. The author does not make his attack on this consciousness a call as immediate as a postman's knock but with that element in the novel not finally caught, though other spells may operate, we are not reading it in the deepest way. And this point of it all, the idea of which the whole piece is the expression, this large rich superior interest to which all the others are contributive, although the whole thing throbs and flushes with it, may remain quite invisible to most because of its being so inferentially and intimately no less than intensely present throughout and its asking therefore a service of extraction; its existing, that is, all beautifully, only as a matter of interpretation. This is to say, in summary, that the novel as its *raison d'être* has a sense of its own, a mystic meaning proper to itself to give out to the participant reader who pushes his way into its distinction, which is behind doors and beyond vestibules, as it were; a beautiful little sense to be taken by the acutest receptivity, the intelligence capable of hospitality to it, and nothing at all to be made of it, as to its essence, by others.

We take offered things in as aspects and visibilities, and the supremely good novels abound in aspects, each a different face of the subject, each contributing to a vew of *all* its dimensions. They have sides and backs, parts in the shade as true as parts in the sun. The multiplication of aspects makes for that "roundness" in which beauty and lucidity largely reside —putting for the beautiful, always, in a work of art, the close, the curious, the deep. The reason, the relation of presented aspects makes for a certain fulness of truth, truth diffused, distributed, and, as it were, atmospheric. The expressive idea or motive, what the novel was done *for*, its message and challenge to intelligent curiosity, comes as an extracted sense of the whole, or as final, as the supreme implication, out of the conflict of its aspects and is interesting as it comes out and by the process and duration of that emergence. Our aftersense shall recognize it as the last thing left on the table, as the *vraie vérité*, the fundamental truth more or less obscurely lurking behind all the rest. It rests altogether with the artist not to break with his values, not to give away his importances. A novel in which nothing is in eclipse, but everything rather straight in evidence, with its whole character in its face, as it were, and its innermost penetralia standing open, doesn't represent the whole sense of any complicated subject, and a novelist's straight or didactic affirmation of his general truth, a bareness instead of a fulness of aspects misses that handsome wholeness of effect of the distinctively rich presentation, is one in which any round and complete embodiment has simply been denied. It is a novel that fails to squeeze out of its subject all that the subject has to give, leaves part of its value unexpressed, and so violates the law of entire expression. All art is expression and is therefore vividness. The novelist's straight or didactic affirmation of his general truth, even his most emphasized personal guarantee or "word of honor" for it, is indeed a crude inartistic substitute for the show. Any main artistic intention is of value but so far as it is visibly brought home to us, brought home by way of an inference we can make for ourselves.

If the prime interest in a novel is its meaning, its idea that the total conveys, we must feel that some general idea *is* represented. A lucid account of any such work involves that identification. We won't take time to push our way through the thick undergrowth of any one of James's final things to arrive at its central object and evaluate it; one remembers, in this connection, that after traversing an antechamber or two and the famous crooked corridor, as the very prize, the sacred presence at the heart of them, H. G. Wells came upon a dead kitten, an eggshell, and a bit of string, where he had rather expected to encounter God himself as their meaning. No matter what the idea is, so long as a novel founds itself upon one for its subject and is expressive of it, every *parcelle* being a weighed and related value, whatever else the work may do or may not do it has acknowledged a principle of composition and contrives at least to hang together, and it is possible to say with exactness what the whole exhibitionally means. An interest has been created and strained clear, giving the work a consistent sustained preserved *tone,* a value in itself, whatever the thinness—which is dependent on the value of what is being demonstrated, the triviality or worth of the general lesson that may seem to us latent in it. The fatal break of tone is the one unpardonable sin for the novelist.

We see everyone and everything but as they are visible in the subject's interest—the interest of its being handed over to us as some communicated closeness of truth. But there are degrees of merit in subjects; there are thankless ones that make petty returns regardless of what the novelist does for them: it's only into thickened motive and accumulated character that the painter of life bites more than a little. If the embodied notion is a joy that has to be fished up, as Truth, from the very bottom of the well, it ought to be intrinsically worth it. The novels we come back to for the sake of what they show us have as their presiding thought and commanding value a potent idea with an intensity of relation to the actual, one that is symbolic and of large application, a pointed warning that it behooves us to heed and remember, a moral perhaps more curious than self-evident, obscure by reason of its consisting of the shy and illusive, the delicate things. They most vividly read to us, all through, the lesson of values, of just appreciation and just proportion—the saving and sacred sense of proportion. And if the value that is most rendered, albeit indirectly, kept indirect in the higher interest, is "internal" it also partakes of the nature of things "eternal." They are comprehensive and searching, rich and complex, the novels we love in the light of what they do for us, educative, formative, fertilizing; they may help us to a better consciousness, to live into a part of ourself previously unvisited and now made accessible as by the sharp forcing of a closed door. The extension of life is the novel's best gift.

If we resort for lights on James to Wells we read that "James has never discovered that a novel isn't a picture . . . He wants a novel to be simply and completely *done*. He wants it to have a unity, he demands homogeneity. Why *should* a book have that? For a picture it's reasonable, because you have to see it all at once. But there's no need to see a book all at once . . . James *begins* by taking it for granted that a novel is a work of art that must be judge by its oneness. Judged first by its oneness . . . The picture, on the other hand, is

forced to a unity because it can see only one aspect at a time.
I am doubtful even about that. Think of Hogarth or Carpac-
cio. But if the novel is to follow life it must be various and
discursive. Life is diversity and entertainment, not completeness and satisfaction. All actions are half-hearted, shot delightfully with wandering thoughts—about something else. All
true stories are a felt of irrelevances. But James set out to
make his novels with the presupposition that they can be
made continuously relevant. And perceiving the discordant
things, he tries to get rid of them. He sets himself to pick
the straws out of the hair of Life before he paints her. But
without the straws she is no longer the mad woman we
love. He talks of 'selection,' and of making all of a novel
definitely *about* a theme," etc. Life, being all inclusion
and confusion, has no direct sense whatever for the subject and is capable of nothing but splendid waste. Art, on
the other hand, is all discrimination and selection, all picking
and composing, in search of the hard latent *value* with which
alone it is concerned. James conceived fiction ever and always
to be the prose-painted *picture* of life, the representation of
subjects drawn from life, and he wanted his subjects to be
able quite definitely to state and declare themselves *as* subjects; and since a picture without composition slights its most
precious chance for beauty he had a horror of two stories,
two pictures, in one; he had a horror of uncontrolled impro-
visation, the unchanneled running on and on of invention;
and he had a love, when it is a question of picture, the
beautiful business of the picture of life, of anything that
makes for proportion and perspective.

James, wrote Wells, "omits everything that demands digres-
sive treatment or collateral statement. For example, he omits
opinions. In all his novels you will find no people with
defined political opinions, no people with religious opinions,
none with clear partisanships or with lusts or whims, none
definitely up to any specific impersonal thing." All life comes
back to the question of our relations with each other. James
saw the novel as a picture of relations and the novelist as
possessive of a richly sophisticated view of relations and a fine
inquisitive speculative sense for them. (And a rich sophistica-

tion, by the way, is after all a gradual growth.) He saw as the real stuff of drama and the natural food of novelists the passions and embroilments of men and women, the free play of character and the sharp revelation of type. He felt himself "after" persons so much more than anything else: the private world, the world of the individual with its touching human values and faint sweet scents of character. Religion, morals, politics, economics, esthetics would be thus, as systematic matter, very well in their place, but quite secondary and subservient. The affair of the painter is not the immediate, it is the reflected field of life, life's subjective concomitants, the tragedy and comedy of life, character, manners, things seen, felt, imagined, states of mind, states of soul: the novelist's general subject in the last analysis is the nature of man; he is a great projector of the human image and the human idea. The moving accident, the rare conjunction, whatever it be, doesn't make the story—in the sense that the story is our excitement, our amusement, our thrill and our suspense; the human emotion and the human attestation, the clustering human conditions we expect presented, only make it. For the "story," that is for the pure pearl of his idea, the novelist has to take a deep, straight dive into the deep sea of a general truth. And his interest in the story *as such* is ever, obviously, overwhelmingly, for the storyteller, one reiterates, the prime and precious thing. "What stories they are!" wrote Wells. "Concentrated on suspicion, on a gift, on possessing a 'piece' of old furniture, on what a little girl may or may not have noted in an emotional situation." The novelist makes his appeal to the interesting, wherever it resides and abides. Neither he nor his reader knows, ideally, until the material has been got into real close quarters with by absolutely ciphering it out, what quantity of importance, under the pressure and the screw, it is susceptible of giving.

The painter's subject consists of the related state, to each other, of certain figures and things. To exhibit these relations is to "treat" his idea, neglecting none of those that directly minister to interest, and omitting all of those that don't. The novelist has a feeling for human relations, as the social climate qualifies, intensifies, generally conditions and colors them. His characters, as figures in a composed picture, live in a medium, since it takes a medium to give them an identity, the medium also enjoying in a like degree the luxury of an existence, and they fail of reality and but swim in the vague and the void and the abstract unless their social conditions, their generative and contributive circumstances, of every discernible sort, enter for all they are worth into the representative attempt: in these facts and in the character of each of the persons involved resides the drama. A certain combination of circumstances produces a situation which is then developed by character interaction, the issue from which makes a drama. To say that for James the novel is a picture of a complexity of relations is hardly to say all. The novelist constitutes his picture in some action, builds his situation round some climax: the idea he wishes to express resolves itself into a progression, the figures in the picture being the agents of the drama. The progress in James's vocation as an artist took a jump rather late in life when, after acquiring mastery of the scenic philosophy and method from the years of his theatrical experiments, he came to know the degree in which the art of the novel profitably comes near that of the drama. He came to see, that is, the utility for a narrative plan of the principle of the scenario, an intensely structural, intensely hinged and jointed preliminary frame as a key that, working in the same *general* way, fits the complicated chambers of both the dramatic and the narrative lock. The beauty of the conception is in the approximation of the divisions, the proportions, and general rhythm of the narrative form to the successive acts of a play. By sticking to the march of an action as a basis of method and drawing up a detailed scenario James got, from point to point, each of the steps of his story, his clear order and expressed sequence, each stage, tint, shade of his subject, every main joint and hinge in its place as unarrested drama, a close march of cause and effect as straight as a play.

The first step of his situation, of his illustrative action that makes the prime idea a subject or a story, places itself exactly where that situation may be conceived as really beginning to show. We become acquainted with the characters dramatically. Everything that concerns us about their conditions and antecedents is given not by the inserted block of merely referential narrative but on the lines of present picture and movement, by the unfolding of the action itself, which of itself involves and achieves all presentation and explanation. Each successive act of a play or book of a novel is a single aspect of the situation, a distinct lamp that illuminates with due intensity one of the subject's faces, a mass of interest "complete in itself," with an individual character of its own, but also carrying in its bosom the completeness of preparation for the one following—which in turn carries in *its* pocket the completeness of preparation for the next, so that everything precedent to the climax consists but in preparation for this momentousness, so that the whole affair is gathered there ready to break. Each division presents its own little question, gives it its development, and deals with it, has its own little climax and *dénouement d'acte* of the right emphasis and promise, the action taking a step in it in its march toward the main climax, that which gathers the action up to a fulness and illuminates or illustrates the subject with force.

The dramatic side of human situations subsists of course on contrast. The situation springs from some sharp antithesis, from the right oppositions, from the play of wildness and the development of extremes. The dramatist is a presenter of conflict and an extractor from contrasted things of their sense or their lesson. We may strike lights by opposing order to order, one sort to another sort; for in that case we get the correspondences and equivalents that make differences mean something; we get the interest and the tension of disparity where a certain parity may have been in question. There is psychological and dramatic interest galore in lively oppositions of sensibility, with the sharpness of each, its special exclusions, its native dangers, well exhibited. But alternative, irreconcilable points of view, as embodied in contrasted figures of different types, are dramatized, played against each other, only when something is made to depend on them, depend on the question at issue, for certain persons who are actors in the story. The struggle, the tension, the "row" enacts itself round a loss or gain, an important interest at stake and hanging in the balance as the concrete form and dramatic value of the question which it is the function of the piece to present and then push to its solution. Of the essence of drama are the questions what will happen, who suffer, who not suffer, what turn will be determined, what crisis created, what issue found? A figure in any picture of a conflict, acting out of his force and his weakness in the face of felt difficulty and danger, has his decisions to make and his consequences to meet. In the tighter squeeze of his crisis there is that which, when it asks of him a proof or a sacrifice, he has to forfeit or forego, thanks to the value he sets on something else. Character, the question of what the novelist's projected and agitated agents should individually, and all intimately and at the core, show themselves, would unmistakeably be the key to his drama, and would indeed make a drama of any sort possible. And a character, too, is interesting as it comes out and by the process and duration of that emergence.

As James entered upon the copious final productions that are the consummation of his distinguished career, and our richest and hugest inheritance of imaginative prose, the august light of a beneficent method was cast upon his path by this conception, borrowed from the drama, of organizing the novel as an action to give it bony structure, to give it *line* on which to string the pearls of detail. It lightened the acute constructional, the endless expressional question, the whole stiff mystery of technique. This is perhaps the place to add, however, that if a person hasn't, for fiction, to some degree the "root of the matter" in him, hasn't the sense of life and the penetrating imagination, no method or system alone will much avail for him. *That* question comes back to the kind and degree of the artist's prime sensibility, which is the soil out of which his subject springs, the quality and capacity of that soil, its ability to "grow" with due freshness and straightness any vision of life.

James in his final phase, at the beginning of his period of consummate mastery and maturity of craftsmanship, one was saying, grew to see both the novelist's and the dramatist's compositional procedures as ruled by the march of an action, the rise, progress, culmination, and solution of a crisis, the essential turns or steps of which, for intensity and sharpness, for the very closest and finest logic, it is well to mark out in advance. The act of a play is a segment of the action during which the attention of the audience is held, unbroken and unrelaxed, throughout the length of a carefully discriminated social occasion in the history and intercourse of the actors concerned, a certain conjuncture of their affairs that places them for the time vividly in relation to each other to advance the action another step. And the novel, too, has for its units or constructional blocks a sequence of thoroughly expressed occasions, architecturally combined, each making a piece of the building and corresponding to the well-marked, well-balanced act structure of the playwright. What a character in a play will say and do during a given social occasion is the result of his or her sense of the situation or sensibility to the crisis, the culmination of processes of vision, feeling, consciousness that have been working within that person. But it is not this act of vision in itself, just what takes place in consequence of it that makes the scene, which is arranged to put this vision to a real and direct test. The objectivity of the dramatist's form prevents him from "going behind" the spoken word to the representation of a character simply motionlessly *seeing*, without leaving a chair and without being approached by another person, as a direct thing in itself, and any attempt to make the still lucidity of this act as "interesting" as, say, the surprise of a caravan or the identification of a pirate. With the directly subjective picturing of an "exciting" inner life, an underlying soul-state, with going behind to compass explanations and amplifications, motives and sentiments, the playwright has nothing whatever to do, committed as he is for everything to the logic of only one way, the scenic way, to characters intensely confronted and talking, to really constructive dialogue, diologue, organic and dramatic, speaking for itself, representing and embodying substance and form.

Dialogue is an "overtreatment," a spinning out, a space-consumer. The definite office of the scene is to express *all that is in* the hour, to report what "passes" on a given crucial occasion closely and completely. Since the dramatist presents the picture of his situation throughout its entirety on absolutely scenic lines, by the arrangement, the organization of dialogue to "speak for itself" copiously and comprehensively, his form is one difficult enough to challenge and inspire great adroitness so soon as the elements to be dealt with begin at all to "size up." The novelist however, thanks to the greater flexibility of his form, has a choice as to treatment of his occasions. Since his subject is of an importance and complexity that, no matter what the science of control or thrift of treatment, declines to enact itself save in terms of amplitude, fortunately for him he is not obliged to hand *all* of it over to the scenic. Indeed with a situation making for developments on any scale, in order to be wise as to length and keep it to a decent compactness, to prevent it from sprawling out over ever so much more ground than he needs for his best effect to cover, nothing is more probable than that he will be able to afford only in a comparatively minor degree to express his action scenically, to express scenically, in fact, only those occasions or parts of an occasion that absolutely insist or cry aloud to be so represented. For the rest there is the fusion and synthesis of picture, "narrative representation" that keeps down the lateral development and aims at those richly summarized and foreshortened effects, a packed and calculated closeness, for which the magician has ever to don his best cap and gown. For flexibility and variety, for effective expressional change and contrast, the novel treats its theme by intensities of foreshortening alternated with vividnesses of extension.

What a man thinks and what he feels are the history and the character of what he does. There is the novelist's interest in personal character and in the "nature" of a mind, of almost any mind the heaving little sea of his subject may cast up. Any situation depends for its interest on the nature of the persons situated, and thereby on their way of taking it; depends, that is, on its aspects, on varying states of vision, of feeling, of consciousness; depends on the analyses made of the situation by its different agents. We want the situation clear but we also want it thick, and we get the thickness in the human consciousness that entertains, that amplifies and interprets it. A person's vision of the aspects, the "related" sides, of a situation is, exactly, his knowledge of it. The different faces of the subject impart a full roundness to the action, the completeness of the drama-quality. The novelist, then, shows the situation best by showing almost exclusively how it is felt, by recognizing as its main interest impressions strongly made and intensely received. The business of the novel and the march of its action, not to say the precious moral of everything, is just the demonstration of this process of vision. The action of a novel is all interior, the play of inward things, mind and attitude, operations of a superficially idle order. The kinds of subjects for the novel and play essentially differ: if the inwardness is of a sort that doesn't become an outwardness effective theatrically then it is not a completely scenic subject, not a subject for stage presentation, but one largely responsive to pictorial treatment. There are relations of an intimacy, really of an obscurity, unappreciable from outside, and for which we need more of an inside view of the nature and working of the mind itself. There are common and covert dangers that "look like nothing," and that can be but inwardly and occultly dealt with, which involve the sharpest hazards to life and honor and the highest instant decisions and intrepidities of action.

Spirtual adventures, experience, is our apprehension and our measure of what happens to us as social creatures—any intelligent report of which has to be based on that apprehension. Without a character's sense of his adventures, his sense *for* them, they may be next to nothing at all: the beauty and the difficulty is just in showing their mystic conversion by that state of being aware into the stuff of story. To enable the reader to know a character intimately and feel with him intensely his adventures, to probe the deeps of human experience and make us understand such obscurities as the motive impelling to a character's actions and the mental process which makes those actions conceivable, no artifice will so serve, for perfect lucidity, for vividness, as the direct picture of the consciousness of the complicated soul, the placing and keeping on exhibition under our eye throughout an occasion of the character's depicted, betrayed, communicated consciousness and picture of that occasion.

A good part of the solution of the "technical," that question of the way of a thing is done, James saw, more and more in his later time, is achieved by the lodging of a mind of some sort, in the sense of a reflecting and coloring medium, within each discriminated occasion, as its center, for the treatment of its interest, and then to let this center, once it is selected and fixed, determine and rule. The novelist who is a novelist sticks to his center, sticks to our knowing the occasion but *through* the particular projected sensibility's knowing it, through his or her faculty of appreciation and delicate vision of evertyhing; and there is no breaking-up of the register, no sacrifice of the recording consistency, that doesn't scatter and weaken. The novelist goes behind this one character, he doesn't go behind the others or the unity of impression goes to smash. The other agents are all, as it were, phenomenal to a particular imagination, and that imagination, with all its contents, phenomenal to the reader. We thus get, by an economy of process interesting in itself, the thoroughly pictured creature and at the same time the equal desideratum, its depicted full fusion with other lives that remain undepicted. The other lives, the rest of the quantity of life, press in, squeeze forward, to the best of their ability; but, restricted as they are to presentation through another mind's power of apprehension of them, through what another person makes of them, they prevail at best by indirectness. No character in a play (any play not a mere monologue) has, for the right expression of the thing, a usurping consciousness; the consciousness of others is exhibited exactly in the same way as that of the "hero" which only takes its turn with that of the other agents of the story, no matter how occasional these may be. What "happens," by that felicity, happens thus to everyone concerned. The references in the playwright's action can only be, with intensity, to each other, to things exactly on the same plane of exhibition with themselves. "Kinds," however, are the very life of literature, and truth and strength come from the complete recognition of them, from abounding to the utmost in their respective senses and sinking deep into their consistency.

Often with the short novel, and sometimes also with the long, the subject is such that a single presented register is equal to the task of giving the whole of it just through the occasions of his or her proximity and attention; is capable of stating to the last ounce of their weight each and all of its occasions as they pass before and touch and affect that individual. The progress and march of the whole in that case becomes and remains that of a single creature's understanding, and the penetration of this understanding the novelist's action and story. Usually, though, the novelist to obtain his best values must proceed by employing a number of successive centers working in arranged alternation, each so established that the portion of the subject framed by the particular point of vision and treated from it will constitute a unit or solid block of wrought material. This planned rotation of aspects is as near an approach to the dramatic as the novel may permit itself: it lends to the novel the charm of the scenic consistency, the consistency of the multiplication of interesting and interested points of view and making them amusingly various; the presentation of those inherent oppositions from type to type in which drama most naturally resides. There is the group-quality of drama: the situation developed by the interactions of the different members of a group upon each other, each of the agents, true to his function, taking up the theme from the other.

The play, as distinguished from the novel, lives exclusively on the spoken word—not on the report of the thing said but, directly and audibly, on that very thing. It is only in the drama that dialogue is constructive. In the novel the report of talk between persons is singularly suicidal from the moment it is not directly illustrative of something given us by another method, something constituted and presented by picture. Picture is a compendium of what a character sees, an artifice by which we enter into his thoughts—which he is the only person to know anything about; we abound in his sense of the situation, we see what he sees for himself in it, his constructive, inferential, divinatory notion of it; the ferment that the swarming, the quite assaulting phenomena have produced in him is laid bare. All the elements of his case are evoked to set the stage, to effectively prepare or overprepare for a scene in which the vision is confirmed and illustrated by something coming of it that justifies and crowns the preparation; a colloquial exchange in which, say, between certain of the characters something is settled because of this vision. The values of a scene flower only on ground that has been solidly laid for them by picture. The novelist will wisely restrict the larger conversational play and use the report of talk between persons only sparingly as a precious and supreme resource, the very flower of illustration of the subject, the thing that can least afford to be cheap. The flower must keep its bloom, or in other words not be too much handled, in order to have a fragrance on just those occasions when nothing but its fragrance will serve. And of course any transaction, any chapter of intercourse, any interview to which our perceptive friend is not a party, a scenic occasion revolving on an improvised pivot of its own, has nothing to do with illustrating the subject. The unity of each aspect as a compact constructional block is preserved only when the scenes within it are kept to this agent and whoever else.

The situation, or part of one, is presented not as the novelist's own impersonal account but as his account of somebody's impression of it—the terms of that person's access to it and estimate of it contributing to intensification of interest, interest enriched *by the way*. There is no economy of treatment without an adopted, a related point of view. Clearness and concreteness depend for any pictorial whole on some concentrated individual notation of them and the novelist has that provision for interest, proceeding from his form, which consists in placing advantageously, placing right in the middle of the light, at the heart of his complexity, an irrepressible appreciation of it, an excited concentrated feeling about it, as the most polished of possible mirrors upon which to represent it as reflected. As his central point of vision he sets up, with conscious craft, to guard his interest, the best point of view from which he can rake his field. The artist must know how he is doing it or he is not doing it at all. He must have a sure perception of where the interest of his subject really lies and he must see sharply the way that most presents that interest as against the ways that comparatively give it away. The distinction between substance and form in a really wrought work of art signally breaks down. The two *discharged* offices are separate before the fact, but the sacrament of execution indissolubly marries them, and the marriage has only to be a "true" one for the scandal of a breach not to show. Form alone takes and holds and preserves substance. The found, because the sought for, form is the guarded citadel and tabernacle of interest.

Since the values are gathered by the light of these intense personal consciousnesses that shine over the field, their predominance being usurped by no other, the novelist will prefer to employ for his central spirits persons of some cleverness and competence rather than those of very simple or common kind. Mere louts, of course, with their gross, dense, helpless stupidity and commonplaceness, need not bother to apply. Doubtless it's in a degree an exclusion and a state of weakness to be without experience of the meaner conditions, the lower manners and types, the ignorance and the vice, but it is better to make a vessel of sensibility upon which the reader is invited to fix his attention and linger over full and rich instead of poor and meager, to make it one with which the reader can feel some kinship or sympathy rather than to make it of a dull, vulgar, shallow capacity. This sensibility is interesting only when no one else is equally so, and carries the interest then with least of a stumble or a sacrifice. The person most worthy of the foreground and the limelight possesses an intellectual and moral substance into which the novelist can cut thick, but he reflects and makes us see the things that interest us most because they interest him so much as the subject of the experience, caught up as he is as a foredoomed, entangled, embarrassed agent in the general imbroglio. He is qualified to form the glass through which we look at the crisis because he is tried, tested, harrowed, and exhibited by that crisis. He has an excited and concentrated feeling about it—and this is the finest side of the subject, the one thrown into highest relief and given all its value, into which we enter fully for its intensity, taking in deeply his sense of things, charged by the intelligence, the curiosity, the passion, the force of the moment, whatever it be, directing him. There is no beautiful report of things on the novelist's part unless a particular detachment has operated. The author never breaks the chain of the projected consciousness to report any matter quite straight and quite shamelessly. He reaches his objective only through the reflective imagination and moral nerves of the troubled life at the center of his subject used as a basis of vision. The interest of everything is all that it is this particular perceiver's vision, conception, interpretation with which all the facts are richly charged and colored. That saturates our sense of them with the character's sense, thanks to which enhancement we get intensity—and without intensity where is vividness, and without vividness where is presentability?

The projection of such a consciousness upon an affair gives us the side on which the subject is strong but his mere personal sense of it taken by itself probably also leaves a part of the value for ourselves, and also for the agitated agent, unexpressed. There is the story of the hero, and then, thanks to the intimate connection of things, the story of the story itself. To confound the object, as the philosophers have it, with the subject, to lose sight of the idea in the vehicle, of the intention in the fable is to misunderstand the nature of art in general. The point of the picture is in the contrast between the two. We take for granted by the general law of fiction a primary author, take him so much for granted that we forget him in proportion as he works upon us, and he works upon us most in fact by making us forget him. His report of people's experience as a storyteller is essentially his appreciation of it, and there is no interest for him in what his hero, his heroine, or any one else does save through that admirable process. As the historian of the matter sees and speaks through others, the reader addicted to seeing "through"—one thing through another—meets him halfway, passive, receptive, appreciative, often even grateful; unconscious, quite blissfully, of any bar to intercourse, any disparity of sense between them. His vision superimposed on the reader's matches. The representation within the work of the double consciousness by insidious proceedings makes the thrill and the curiosity—and no one was more adept at this than James: it was his "special line of goods," the flower at its finest, and grown as nowhere else. There is nothing else in literature quite like the fruits of his finest artistry. Moreover, his mass of work is wholly unequalled, considering the quality of his show, by any other eminent abundance. He was to leave the novel a far other and vastly more capacious and significant affair than he found it, and he did not shrink from calling it, under the right persuasion, the most independent, most elastic, most prodigious of literary forms.

BIBLIOGRAPHY

THE person who knew most of James's secrets, and who was also best able to keep them to herself, was the late Edna Kenton. At least I am inclined to believe so and to estimate her critical-scholarly contributions as more valuable and various and communicated on a higher level than anyone else's. Representative of her quality is the essay, "Henry James to the Ruminant Reader: *The Turn of the Screw*," published in *Arts*, November 1924.

The fullest and best essay on *The Turn of the Screw* is the late Harold C. Goddard's, published in *Nineteenth-Century Fiction*, June 1957, but written many years earlier. (Goddard has written a major critical work, an exceedingly fine book, *The Meaning of Shakespeare*, published by the University of Chicago Press in 1941.)

The most diligent scholar of James at present is Leon Edel. An admirable *Bibliography of Henry James* by Leon Edel and Dan H. Laurence was published by Rupert Hart-Davis in London in 1957.

The revised version of Edmund Wilson's famous essay on Henry James is in *The Triple Thinkers,* published in 1948 by the Oxford University Press. It is to this discussion of the ambiguity by America's leading critic that I owe my introduction to James.

The writings of F.R. Leavis, England's foremost critic, on James, are of considerable interest. Essays by Leavis on James are in two of his books, *The Great Tradition* and *The Common Pursuit,* both published by Chatto & Windus in London and in New York by George W. Stewart. Leavis's periodical *Scrutiny* was the best of the literary quarterlies and also the one that contained the most interesting criticism of James.

A notable essay, "Henry James and the Trapped Spectator," by L.C. Knights, the distinguished critic of Shakespeare, is in his book *Explorations*, published in 1947 by Chatto & Windus in London and by George W. Stewart in New York.

Another notable essay, "Appearance and Reality in Henry James," by Marius Bewley appeared in *Scrutiny* and was reprinted in his book *The Complex Fate*, published by Chatto & Windus in London in 1952.

The late A.R. Orage, who was acquainted with James, wrote several short occasional pieces on him. "Henry James and the Ghostly," published in the *Little Review*, August 1918, is representative.

In Defense of Reason by Yvor Winters, published by the Swallow Press & William Morrow in 1947, contains an essay on James of some interest.

F.W. Dupee's *Henry James*, in the American Men of Letters Series, published by William Sloane Associates in 1951, is as good as any of the previous book-length studies of him, and is available since 1956 in a paperback edition as a Doubleday Anchor Book.

In the Cage and Other Tales, The Ambassadors, The Awkward Age, and *What Maisie Knew* are available in Anchor paperback editions.

The Grove Press has in print *The Golden Bowl* and *The Sacred Fount*.

The Wings of the Dove, The Turn of the Screw, The Bostonians, The Portrait of a Lady, and *Washington Square* are all in Random House's Modern Library. A volume of James's short stories is in the Modern Library Giant series.

The Spoils of Poynton and *The Other House* are published by New Directions. *The Princess Casamassima* is published by Macmillan.

Rupert Hart-Davis in London publishes *The Tragic Muse, The Reverberator*, and also the English edition of numerous other works by James.

The Prefaces written by James to his New York editions have been collected under the title *The Art of the Novel*, and are in print by Scribner in cloth and paperback editions.